# AC/SU

A history of the North Dakota Agricultural College
and North Dakota State University in photographs

Richard Chenoweth

Mark Strand

Design by Heather Lindsay Strand

Library of Congress Catalog Number 84-61566

ISBN 0911042-30-x

©1985
North Dakota Institute for Regional Studies
Fargo

# Images of resilience, humanity, vitality

The impression I got in paging through this handsome collection of photographs was of the great sense of vitality and humanity that NDSU represents—generations of people striving to improve their own lot in life, and, in doing so, enriching the lives of others.

In a sense, I suppose a university community is the outside world in microcosm, with all the joys, disappointments, triumphs and frustrations people everywhere experience, to greater or lesser degrees. Yet it is different.

Because most of the people are young, full of physical vitality, self confidence and hope, a university is a livelier, more optimistic place than the world outside the gates. Not so tired, worldly and blase. Because of that it's an exciting place to live and work. The pictures in this book capture that excitement, better than words.

A university is a hotbed of positive thinking—by the students because they are young; by the faculty because university professors, whatever their philosophical stripe, tend to be idealists. They believe humanity can be improved, and they are the ones who plant the seeds.

Down through its history, NDAC/NDSU has experienced feast and famine—famine more often than feast, I'm afraid—periods of relative tranquility; periods of internal strife; attacks from those who would seek to destroy it, or at least bring it to its institutional knees. But it has survived those and prospered—physically, spiritually, intellectually and technically—and the world is better because of that. North Dakota and the world have the people in these pictures to thank for that. Now deeply rooted in the onetime wheat field from which it sprang nearly a century ago, simultaneously nurturing and drawing its strength from the state and its people, NDSU is a powerful positive influence on the quality of people's lives.

Recently, a set of figures was brought to my attention, that as of Commencement 1984, NDSU had graduated a total of 39,438 persons, 30,148 of them since it became a university in 1960. It is clear from those figures that NDSU experienced its most dramatic physical growth during the past quarter century. With nearly 10,000 students currently enrolled, it has become one of the state's larger urban communities. I feel that reflects very well on the institution's viability. It is clearly fulfilling a need. Unfortunately, some of that closeness and humanity that existed in the days of the Waldrons, Ladd, Putnam, Arvold, and Shepperd who figure so prominently in the photographs of its formative years has fallen victim to that growth. In a community of 12,000 people in a much more mobile time, a certain amount of impersonality inevitably occurs.

Yet there is still, to my mind, something very special about this place. As its founders intended I am sure, it remains open to virtually all who would seek to improve their lot in life. It provides them a stimulating environment within which to nurture their talents and pursue their dreams. NDSU has never discriminated on the basis of wealth, social standing, religion, sex, race, or creed. Therein lies the wellspring of its great vitality.

Understandably, as NDSU's geometric growth began to occur, the involvement of people in all of its facets grew accordingly. An alumni organization, which had been almost the private preserve of a handful of loyal Fargoans, became nationwide in scope, involving thousands among some 40,000 current alumni, former students and friends. A stalwart band of sports fans, who had weathered the 0-10 seasons of the early 1960s formed the nucleus of today's avid Team Maker organization, which numbers well up in the hundreds. A Development Foundation, formed in the late 1960s, piloted the institution through its first significant fundraising campaign. Project SU'75 substantially enhanced the University's physical facilities.

Today NDSU is a strong, vital university, undoubtedly the strongest it has ever been. An institution in which all of its builders, down through the years, can take justifiable pride.

At the moment, NDSU and North Dakota are again experiencing a period of lean economic times. It may be nip and tuck trying to maintain the forward momentum NDSU has enjoyed over the past quarter century. We must strive mightily to avoid slipping back and losing ground.

Fortunately, throughout its history, the institution has shown immense resilience in dealing with exigencies of various types. Barring some sort of total economic collapse of the U.S. economy, I'm confident NDSU will survive and prosper.

That confidence is rooted in the institution's heritage. One needs only to page through this book to get a feeling for the toughness and exuberance that has characterized NDAC/NDSU and for that matter, the state of North Dakota down through its history. Because of its land-grant mandate, NDSU has been in partnership with the people of North Dakota in coping with the problems that beset us all. That won't change. The school and the state can take pride in what that partnership has achieved.

L.D. Loftsgard
President
May 1, 1985

# How to read this book
**Steve Ward, class of '63**

In the first place, you probably shouldn't start here. Thumb through the whole book, fan the pages, examine a photograph here and there, check to see if your name is in the index, scan the timelines and headlines, guess at the deep structure. Play with it. Remember the people you knew, the things you did, and the places you saw when you were on campus. Then come back and we'll compare stories, for this book is a sure-fire story-starter.

I can't get past page 20 without grins and anecdotes. That's my grandfather in the second row, second from the right, looking half my age. Over on page 15 he appears again, fencing with Bob Reed who has now turned into a building—Reed-Johnson Dorm. They were among the first graduates in 1895, but in a larger sense they never left.

I can remember in the 40's slewing about in my grandfather's car as he raced across the Minnewaukan flats in pursuit of errant livestock. I was often covered with weeds that flew with each bounce into the air and blew in the cyclone created by our wild chasing. The weeds were part of Grandfather's semi-permanent collection, along with veterinary tools, a chamberpot full of fence staples, and dried flakes of manure, gift of the last calf he'd hauled up to the farmyard for doctoring and my grandmother's disapproval. Eventually, he'd sack up the weeds and ship them off to the college for identification and advice—in their disposal if noxious, in their culture if palatable. The AC lived on in our family.

Those early students were pioneers. College attendance was chancy; sometimes, with stop-outs for work, it took years of determination to finish school. They were creating a tradition where none existed. Barns, buildings, even the city of Fargo burned to the ground, and the Spanish-American War and WW I took boys to the front. Still, they grew. In 1907, A.G. Arvold moved in on the AC the way P.T. Barnum moved in on Bridgeport. He was a promoter, A.G. was, and he'd stage a pageant at the drop of a buskin or a banquet on any occasion, including the inauguration of President Taft, no small eater himself. In 1913 he got up the Student Life Special Train with its motto "Our State Is Our Campus" and sent it out on the N.P. and Great Northern to show off the college and its students. And to eat. The train had a dining car staffed by home economics students.

That extension mission, the mandate and the eagerness to carry the college beyond the classroom, off the campus, out to the people, is what distinguishes a land-grant college like the AC from the more root-bound "halls of ivy." The AC had roots throughout the state.

Clearly, for me, the state, the AC, and my family are all wound up together. The stories that grow out of this page-turning—the pictures in this book of people, places, and events, the quotations from the **Spectrum,** Dick Chenoweth's timelines and cutlines, Mark and Heather Strand's editing and design—this essay is just one person's musing. I think of you looking through the book with me and telling your own stories, the very best sort of coffee-table conversation. Now you tell one, then we'll go on.

By the 30's, when my father and mother attended the AC, the college was entering a lusty maturity, or at least a romantic coming-of-age. I grew up hearing about those years. For instance, Eli Huffman of Minnewaukan, my father's roommate, recalls being awakened by Dad returning late from a date. "I heard a ruckus, got up and looked out in the hallway, and here came Steve up the stairs. He was tearing the wooden slats out of the bannister, tossing them away, muttering, 'She loves me, she loves me not.' " Or Jessie Phillips remembering my parents: "He sat right behind her in class and played with her ringlets. It seemed like inattention to me." Or Dad on the subject of discipline in his fraternity: "Any of the pledges got in trouble, they had to come up to my room and I'd read romantic poetry to them for an hour. Hard case, *two* hours. Man, they toed the line." Or my other grandfather, Andy Thull (who worked with Bob Thorson, now turned into a building—Thorson Maintenance Center), telling my father about a professor who got so agitated reading a love poem that "He cried! Think of it! Actually cried!" Ah, those were romantic times.

They were hard times, too. Students had to be inventive to get to school at all, money being so scarce. My father hauled potatoes home from the valley and sold them for tuition money. Many, including my Aunt Imogene, had to drop out to work; later, others left to fight in WW II. The faculty got into it, too. The Great Purge of 1937-38 turned the administration upside down. On another front, the story is that Leonard Sackett, jailed for participating in a labor rally in Moorhead, had to be bailed out to meet his classes. I imagine him triumphant and unrepentant, quoting Shelley.

Leonard Sackett hasn't turned into a building, yet, but he has turned into a legend. Although he gleefully corrected people who called him *Dr.* Sackett (he never bothered to complete a Ph.D.), he had the thorough discipline and mind-boggling knowledge of the true scholar. If he was prepared, he expected his students to be prepared, and woe to the sluggard. "You there, in the third row. Yes, you. Was Ozymandias a tyrant? You haven't read the poem? You can read, can't you?" Sackett was rumored to be particularly tough on women; my Aunt Claire avoided his class for years, then found him most gracious when she worked up the nerve to enroll. Actually, he was tough on everyone, so everyone learned, out of a sense of self-preservation if nothing else.

Students and faculty did double-duty in those years, working and going to school, holding down extra jobs to support the love of teaching. Mr. Sackett read poetry on WDAY-radio, acted in community theater plays (reviewed for the **Fargo Forum** by his colleague Francis Schoff), collected memoirs and diaries for the Institute for Regional Studies. He even laid bricks: after the '57 tornado, he rebuilt his own house.

Which brings us to the last section of the book, 1948-1985, during which the AC became SU. Perhaps this is your era as it is mine and my son's. What memories are triggered by this time of the Korean War, the Four Professors, and Viet Nam? By the incredible building program including the Library, Memorial Union, the new pharmacy building, the Little Country Theatre's move to Askanase Hall, and the death and resurrection of Festival Hall? By the names of the **Spectrum** editors, student presidents, and **Bison Annual** editors? By the football teams and homecoming queens, by the roommates and Saturday night dates at the Old YMCA before it blew away from the corner of 12th Avenue and 13th Street before it changed its name to University Drive? I came to SU in 1960 quoting Robert Frost: "Home is where, when you go there, they have to take you in." They did; I've been here ever since. My wife and son and I moved into married students' housing: Silver City, highest birth rate in the state, now a parking lot. There were 3,000 students then, now there are 9,000. The campus Carnegie Library was the music building, the present music building was Minard parking lot, and the parking lot at Second and Roberts was the Fargo Carnegie Library. It was a time of change.

The campus was growing up. The students were rebellious in the 60's, staging protests and teach-ins, rejecting Clyfford Still's paintings, zipping to Zap. Later, they would turn street-wise and jaded as they returned from Viet Nam. But usually, they were hard-working, vocationally-inclined, conservative.

No professor represents all three eras for me so well as O.A. Stevens. He's turned into a building, of course—Stevens Hall, cradle of biological sciences—another example of that strange metamorphosis that occurs on this campus. Dr. Stevens had come to the AC in 1909; his daughter and my mother had been friends since they were children; he had written definitive works on a range of subjects in life science; and in 1964, there he stood beside my desk when I returned from class, as startling as a summons from the president, eager to point out a misplaced comma he'd found in an article he was reading. "Isn't that disgraceful?" he said. "All that work to gather data, then ruin it with punctuation." No job too small for Dr. Stevens. Often, he would patrol the campus to keep students from short-cutting across the grass. Now, that's attention to detail. Add that conservative stewardship to the promotional flair of A.G. Arvold and the versatile flamboyance of Leonard Sackett and you have what tickles me about this book: memories of the people in it.

I'll hush now and let you read. But let me warn you: if there's one other person to listen, you'll never get through **AC/SU.** Like me, you'll never want to.

## Authors' statement

This book represents an attempt to tell in pictures and a few words the story of the North Dakota Agricultural College from its beginning to the State University it is today. We intended to produce a "coffee-table" book, that is a book that alumni and friends will keep nearby as a ready reference.

The timelines came almost exclusively from the student-produced **Spectrum** and admittedly contain a student bias. The short essays contain material from William Hunter's **Beacon Across the Prairie,** the **Spectrum** and other publications of the Communications Office.

Our research found certain themes constant in the University's history. While the method to achieve it has not always been constant, NDSU has maintained that its purpose is to afford a "liberal and practical education for the industrial classes in the several pursuits and professions of life." Other themes include 1) continuity in student life, both in fun and serious preparation for life, 2) a close tie with politics, 3) crowded classrooms and the need for office space, 4) very active programs in music, drama and debate, 5) a national reputation in chemistry and agronomy, 6) a sports program which varied in quality but in which defeating its rival to the north was the measurement of success, 7) an active Extension Service, meeting the needs of the farmer and 8) the importance of individual, in solving crucial issues and providing leadership.

It was impossible to include all events, faculty and students who make the University what it is today. Instead, we hope when paging through it, there will be a few "Ah Hah," "I remember that," and even "I wonder why they did not include. . ."

RC

## Acknowledgments

We wish to acknowledge Dean Archer Jones of the College of Humanities and Social Sciences and Jerry Richardson, Director of Communications and University Relations for conceiving the idea of this book and for giving us the time and resources to bring it to publication.

Mrs. Joanne Jones provided valuable editorial and proofreading services. Professor Steve Ward consulted on nearly every aspect of the book. University Archivist, John Bye, spent hours retrieving both textural and photographic materials. Professors Bill Reid and Warren Kress shared their extensive knowledge of the history of NDAC/SU.

Neal Lambert assisted in the photo research and Gordon Evenson provided darkroom work. Typesetting was by Lisa Baumler with additional proofreading by Kathy Laid.

A considerable number of photographs in this book were made by anonymous photographers to whom we are indebted. Special acknowledgment to the following photographers whose work carried their name:

Daniel Anderson
Lowell J. Anderson
Everett Brust
Don C. Christensen
Roy Corbett
R.M. Erwin
Gordon Evenson
Photo by Flegel
Gillespie Studio
Helen Gunderson
Gary Grinaker
George Hagen
Dean Hanson
Walter Junkin
Nick Kelsh
Neal Lambert
Jim Marsh
Pat McKenrick
Jim Murray
Robert Nelson
Merle E. Nott
Cal Olson
Richard C. Olson
Larry Phillips
Jerry Richardson
Mark Strand

# Contents

# Logrolling on the Prairie: The AC Comes to Fargo

"The bill seems to be drawn with care and skill," the Fargo *Daily Argus* reported. When John E. Haggart introduced Senate Bill 140 at the first meeting of the North Dakota State Legislature, January 20, 1890, he intended it "to provide for the Establishment, Erection and Operation of the North Dakota Agriculture College and Agriculture Experiment Station at Fargo." Providing for the organization of the college and a board of directors, the bill also gave the board the authority to secure temporary quarters and to appoint a faculty. On March 8 the governor signed the bill which, though it appropriated no money, supplied the means for securing federal funds.

Justin Morrill

The Morrill Land-Grant Act of 1862 awarded 120,000 acres of land as well as $15,000 to states with a land-grant institution. Increased by $1,000 a year for a decade, the money would thereafter continue at $25,000 annually. Justin Morrill had wanted to establish "People's Colleges." As opposed to the universities modeled after the private institutions of the East, land-grant universities would combine the liberal education with the vocational, the federal culture.

With the signing of Haggart's bill, several years of controversy over the college's location, the placement of the state capital, and the site for other state institutions came to an end. When the Dakota territorial

legislative session had met in 1883, several members drew lots for the university, an agricultural college, the penitentiary, and the "insane hospital." George Walsh of Grand Forks won and chose the university, Samuel Roberts of Fargo decided on the penitentiary and agricultural college, and Johnston Nicheus of Jamestown received the "insane hospital." Later Nicheus sponsored a bill that gave the penitentiary to Bismarck. During the last days of the session, when the lawmakers enacted measures creating the institutions at the agreed-upon locations, they made no appropriation for the agricultural college.

Not everyone in Fargo felt enthusiasm for Roberts's choice. While a small group of politicians believed the acquisition of any institution would make Roberts too powerful politically, others questioned the wisdom of having two colleges in the same town. Fargo College, a private institution sponsored by the Congregational Church and chartered in 1882, planned to open in 1884.

During the remainder of the decade politicians of Dakota Territory assessed and reassessed the wisdom of establishing an agricultural college in Fargo. Attempting to appropriate money to start the college, D.H. Twomey of the Territorial Council and T.M. Pugh of the House introduced bills in 1885 that called for $45,000 to construct a building.

Walsh requested $250,000 for the university at Grand Forks and testified that the state did not need an agricultural college. Other members from the West indicated their displeasure with the establishment of all the institutions on the east side of the territory, adding that there were already too many schools.

Although the bill passed, with a lesser amount, Governor Gilbert Pierce vetoed it, his veto message endorsing these arguments:

The educational institutions supported by the territory are already too numerous and are taxing the people for their completion and maintenance without any adequate return. The University of North Dakota, located at Grand Forks, is but eighty miles from the proposed location of this new institution, and if the latter is started, a rivalry will necessarily ensue not conducive to the welfare or advantage of either.

The Legislature upheld the veto.

Although the agricultural college was not discussed for the next three or four years, the issue came up at the last territorial legislative session in 1889. Once again location became the problem, this time other cities claiming the college. Attempting to locate the agricultural college in his hometown, on January 14 Hugh McDonald introduced a bill removing the institution from Fargo to Valley City. Subsequently, on January 18 Edwin McNeil, after sponsoring sponsoring a bill placing the college at Casselton, said Casselton promised 160 acres and $10,000 in bond. On

January 30, Smith Stimmel of Fargo introduced a bill to retain the college in his town.

Fargo, which had earlier lost other institutions and most recently the constitutional convention, saw, as one newspaper editor wrote, "a plum of the legislative tree drop into the hats held by rival cities. Fargo, lulled to sleep, awakened only when the proposed college [was] put on wheels, [and] run out of Fargo in search of a city wide-awake enough to build."

Because the legislators had to choose between Fargo and Valley City, committees from both houses considered the two bills with the Council appointing a committee to visit the two towns and make a recommendation. Following the vote of a House committee for Valley City, Fargo sent a delegation to Bismarck, the delegation managing to irk key figures by neglecting the political courtesy of visiting committee leaders before other persons. On February 15 the *Daily Argus* reported in its headlines "War Raging Over Location of the Agricultural College—Fargo Leading." The delegation may have overestimated its impact, for the next day the paper announced that the committee had recommended in favor of Valley City. After the entire Council supported the report of the committee, ten days later, on February 28, the House followed the Council and enacted a measure relocating the college in Valley City by a 32-8 vote.

Once again Fargo sent a delegation to Bismarck, but this time a more politically astute group who successfully persuaded Governor Church to veto the act. The state constitutional convention, planning to meet in Grafton July 4 through August 17, would decide the site for the agricultural college as well as other public institutions. Lobbying for their constituents, interest groups dominated the convention in their efforts to acquire a public institution. Much of the struggle centered on the location of the capital, the legislators considering three cities. In exchange for Bismarck's support, the Fargo delegation favored Bismarck. The Grand Forks group claimed the capital as well as the agricultural college, a school of mines, and a training school combined with the university, while Jamestown hoped for a compromise choice.

When H.F. Miller, earlier a candidate for president of the convention, was elected chairman of the Committee on Public Institutions and Buildings, Fargo's chances for obtaining the college increased. The committee made its report August 7, 1889:

State Capital - Bismarck, Agricultural College - Fargo, State University and School of Mines - Grand Forks, Normal School - Valley City, School for the Deaf and Dumb - Devils Lake, Reform School - Mandan, Normal School - Mayville, State Hospital - Jamestown, Soldiers Home - Lisbon, School for the Blind - Pembina, Industrial School - Ellendale, School of Forestry - Bottineau, School of Science - Wahpeton

Ten days later, on a motion by Miller, the convention adopted the whole report of the committee by a 45 to 28 vote.

The vote did not please everyone in Fargo. While some feared that a "cow college" would never amount to anything, others suggested that "it would be better to go for something of greater benefit, an Indian school, or a school for the deaf and dumb, or a school of science, something big." During the first decade of the century, it would appear that those persons who feared the college would never amount to anything were correct. Between 1890 and 1910, the "Insane Asylum" in Jamestown received $1,127,000 in support from direct taxes while the University in Grand Forks received $950,000 and the Agricultural College received $644,000.

# The Early Years : 1890-1920

"The Board of Trustees of the North Dakota Agricultural College - whatever that is - met yesterday and elected a faculty - whatever that is." Thus Major Alonzo Edwards, editor of the Fargo *Daily Argus*, described the first meeting October 15, 1890. Had he looked at Senate Bill 140, Edwards would have known that the Board, consisting of five members, had the authority to hire and fire all the institution's employees and prescribe their duties.

In specifying the obligations of the faculty, the measure stated that they had the responsibility to adopt a program that embraced a wide area of study but especially in the "application of science and the mechanic arts to practical agriculture." Further, they must develop "rules and regulations for the government and discipline of the college. . . including those that were necessary for the preservation of morals, decorum and health."

Despite Edwards's apparent lack of enthusiasm for what transpired at the meeting on October 15, 1890, most people accept that date as the founding of NDAC. On that day the Board confirmed Dr. Horace E. Stockbridge as President and Director of the Experiment Station. Thirty-three years old, with a Ph.D. from the University of Goettingen, Germany, and four years experience in Japan, Stockbridge came from Purdue University where he had worked for a year as director of the experiment station.

The Board also approved Stockbridge's first appointments to the faculty. Twenty-four-year-old Claire Bailey Waldron became professor of arboriculture. Later he served as Dean of Agriculture and was with NDAC a total of fifty years. Henry L. Bolley, who was the same age as Waldron and remained at NDAC until 1946, was named professor of botany and zoology. Thirty-one-year-old Edwin Ladd, who became professor of chemistry, later served as President of the College until his retirement in 1921. Collectively the three men served NDAC for 137 years.

Had Edwards thought about it, he might have asked what students are. Of the thirty that enrolled for the first term of January 1891, most today would qualify as SOTA, Students Older Than Average— their ages averaged twenty-seven. As winter students, they would not necessarily pursue a four-year degree. Fall enrollment did not reach that number until 1897 and finally broke 100 in September of 1905. By the end of the early years, 1920, fall enrollment, not including high school and short-course students, totaled 375.

In January 1892, leaving their temporary home at Fargo College, the students and faculty moved to a new campus north of Fargo. Consisting of only one building sitting on the open prairie, the College soon boasted other buildings, including a dormitory. Although they paid no tuition at first, students did have other costs, including room and board, estimated in 1891 to be between $117 and $214 for a year.

Politics, as it had in NDAC's founding, continued to play an important role. When President Stockbridge became involved in a political struggle within the Republican Party, the Board fired him in 1893, appointing J.B. Power, secretary of the Board of Trustees, acting President until 1895.

John Henry Worst owed his appointment as President in 1895 to his defeat in the race for re-election as lieutenant governor, receiving the presidency of NDAC instead. Recognizing the talent already at NDAC, Worst, a fine administrator, found good additional people. Able to talk to the people, he did much to gain acceptance, by the farmers of the state, of the scientific work and development being accomplished at NDAC.

Under Worst, the institution became a college in fact, growing during his twenty-one years from 29 students in 1895 to 216 in 1916. Enrollments ran higher in the winter when farmers came to study the "Short Courses." Adept at dealing with the legislature,

Worst obtained funds for programs, faculty, and buildings.

The Experiment Station made great strides during Worst's administration. Henry Bolley, for example, became known as the "Conqueror of Flax Wilt," and worked on such problems as potato scab and wheat rust. C.B. Waldron investigated insect control, made a collection of North Dakota grasses, and landscaped parks and campuses. L.R. Waldron, a plant breeder, helped establish the hardiness of Grimm alfalfa and wheat. Edwin Ladd, who labored on several projects including a crusade for pure food and paint testing, became an international expert on bleached flour and was often called upon to testify in court on its merits. John Shepperd worked on both plant and cattle breeding, winning a gold medal at the Paris World Exposition in 1900 and a grand championship at the Chicago International Livestock Show. Leunis Van Es discovered a tuberculin test for avian tuberculosis as well as a serum to prevent hog cholera. Most importantly, during Worst's administration the educational message was carried to the farmers.

Presiden Worst, who came to NDAC as a result of politics, went out for the same reason. When the Republicans who had placed Worst in power lost out, a new group of people took over control of the legislature.

Edwin Ladd, acceptable to the faculty and students, became President. Although some thought the appointment was temporary, Ladd did not and he retained the position until his election to the United States Senate by the Non-Partisan League in 1920. Ladd's administration encountered complications brought on by the politics that had made him President—and by World War I. By draft or enlistment, students and faculty entered the military service. Ladd's presidency also saw the construction of a new building, Dakota Hall, and the formation of the Student Army Training Corps program.

A good scientist and a great publicist, Ladd, as a head administrator, was often arbitrary and dogmatic both with faculty and students. At a time when fashions were changing, he still attempted to enforce a no-smoking ban on the entire campus. To the delight of the smokers Ladd's successor, Dr. John Coulter, was often seen with a cigar.

# A Timeline: The Early Years

## 1890

**July 19** C.B. Waldron, botanist, reports for duty. For the next three months he is the only member on the staff at the College.

**August 7** The Board of Trustees offers the position of President and Director of the Experiment Station to H.E. Stockbridge, a chemist from Purdue University, at a salary of $2,500.

## 1891

**Fall** Additional faculty this year include Edward S. Keene, University of Illinois, professor of engineering and physics, and W.M. Hays, "Agriculturalist" at the Experiment Station. Mrs. Hays offers a course in domestic science at the farmhouse at the corner of Tenth Avenue and Seventh Street to fifty-six women.

## 1892

**January** The students and faculty move from Fargo College to their new home on the northern outskirts of Fargo. College Hall (Old Main) contains classrooms, offices, and laboratories for the faculty, an office for the President, a room for the library, and an uncompleted upper floor used as a gymnasium. The new campus, with one building and devoid of trees and shrubbery, could be reached by following "Broadway north to Tenth Avenue, then follow the sidewalk west and north to the college. During the dry weather the wheeling is good directly west from the north end of the pavement on Broadway." During the winter months, the "Black Maria," a college bus, is available "for the accommodation of the lady students only."

**May** The first catalog is issued, announcing a winter course of three months each for two years open to anyone fifteen years and over, a preparatory course for persons not ready for recular college work, and a regular four-year course leading to a bachelor of science degree.

**Winter Moorhead Daily News** describes a bobsled party, at a farm north of town, that lasted from 6 p.m. to 4 a.m. Guests included "the faculty of NDAC and their ladies."

## 1893

**Fall** The student body consists of 62 students: 6 juniors, 2 sophomores, 12 freshmen, 41 preparatory class (high school), and 1 special student. The faculty has 12 members.

## 1894

**Fall** Faculty fight pay-reduction move; they feel that there is mismanagement of the funds. The work of the faculty and administration results in a salary schedule and a budget.

**Fall** Chapel, which is compulsory, meets daily and is addressed by the President or faculty at least three times a week.

## 1895

**June 25** Robert Reed, Merton Field, Charles Hall, John Hilborn, and Ralph Ward receive bachelor of science degrees at NDAC's first commencement.

## 1896

**December Spectrum** begins a monthly publication with C.O. Follett, '98, the editor.

## 1897

**January 4** Winter short course begins for twelve weeks, covering different systems of farming, diversified, single, stock raising, and dairy. Lectures are delivered by Professors Bolley, Waldron, and Ladd. Cost, matriculation $2.00, room and board per week $3.00.

**February Spectrum** reports that "A bill was introduced in the legislature a short time ago by one of our North Dakota representatives making the playing of football, or taking any part whatever in the game, a criminal offense. His bill was not as popular as the game and was downed as soon as it was put in play."

**March 6-12** School is closed "on account of the high water in the vicinity of the College and unfavorable conditions of the roads."

**April 24** NDAC's baseball team plays Moorhead Normal, losing 24-23; "The umpire helped the Normalities." May 1 the team plays the faculty and wins 31-15.

**Fall** The Armory (Festival Hall) is completed and ready for use.

**October** Students living at the dormitory have excellent opportunities for study; they are not permitted to go downtown after 7 p.m. without special permission from the matron.

**November** Faculty adopts resolution to take effect January 1 making military drill compulsory for all male students except seniors.

**December** Bulletin No. 30 of the Experiment Station represents the work of three years' experiments on potatoes.

## 1898

**February Spectrum** notes that "The young ladies are taking an active part in athletic sports. Two basketball teams have been organized and the captains are endeavoring to arrange for games with the 'sisters' of Fargo College."

**June** Fifteen boys (later twenty-three) join the army at the outbreak of the Spanish American War and take with them "the vitality of the whole college. The war has killed athletics, crippled society work and caused the students to lose all interest in their regular work."

**Fall** James J. Hill brings farmers to the Experiment Station free; Northern Pacific offers trip for one-half cent per mile.

## 1899

**February** The Department of Bacteriology is busy examining water for sanitary purposes. Two wells from the Carl Piper farm contained typhoid in abundance. The previous year there were five cases of typhoid in the Piper family, including two deaths.

**June 21** Candidates at commencement for B.S. are B.F. Meinecke and L.R. Waldron; Merton Field completes the requirements of a M.S. degree. (The master's degree was formally established in 1900.)

**June** L.R. Waldron, '99, appointed assistant in botany. Later he attends Cornell and Michigan to complete a doctorate.

**October** Editor of the **Spectrum** notes that October 31 is Halloween and that he hopes that no one "will carry his practical jokes beyond reason. Removing bridges or sidewalks . . .is very dangerous." Later it was reported that the women turned out and serenaded the faculty and it was "sad to relate the faculty failed to appreciate their musical ability."

**October** The Biology Department receives nearly $200 worth of supplies and apparatus which will put the department in good shape for the year's work.

**November** The Domestic Economy Department purchases a refrigerator "in which to place the necessities of life."

**December** The Mechanical Department notes that the coal industry of North Dakota has been creating considerable interest of late "owing to a discovery by means of which vast veins of lignite coal. . .may be converted into a fuel said to be equal to the best eastern coal."

**December Spectrum** criticizes the Library and the lack of anyone in charge of buying books. In particular, it notes that the Library does not have **The Origin of Species** and **The Descent of Man.**

## 1900

**January 15** According to the **Spectrum,** during the "short days the college clocks have been turned back 15 minutes to accommodate the late risers."

**Sept 17** Edith Hill, senior, former editor of the **Spectrum,** member of the Athenian Society, student leader, dies of appendicitis. An earlier women's organization is renamed for her; the organization becomes the Edith Hill Young Women's Christian Association.

## 1901

**January 15** American Beauty roses can be secured at the College greenhouse, free of charge. "If the gardener is not there. . .just help yourself."

**January 15** The enrollment almost reaches four hundred for the winter quarter. "The mechanical building is crowded to its utmost capacity. The shops are used eight hours each day. Classes are held in the chapel, reading room and gym."

**Fall** Football team has 8-0 record, outscoring its opponents 280-17 and winning the Phelps Trophy Cup. Two hundred twenty Fargoans take the special train to Grand Forks; both passengers and train are decked

out in green and yellow. NDAC defeats UND, 17-11.

## 1902

**June 11** Commencement is held at the Fargo Opera House. A class of four, Miss Aldyth Ward, Tom Osgood, H.B. Schmidt, and J.F. Jensen, receive the degree of bachelor of science.

**Fall** New staff for the year include Leunis Van Es, Veterinary Science; Haile Chisholm, instructor in blacksmithing; and Edward B. Cochems, graduate of the University of Wisconsin where he played football, baseball, and track and was considered a scholar, assumed the duties of the athletic director. His team goes undefeated, including the UND game, 47-0.

## 1903

**April** Professor Henry Bolley receives a federal commission to visit Europe and the Orient to study flax and its diseases. He leaves for Russia June 1.

**April** The Board of Trustees establishes a Department of Music and elects Dr. C.S. Putnam director.

**November** The band has 30 members - nine clarinets, five cornets, six altos, two tenors, two trombones, one baritone, three basses, and two drums.

**November** NDAC has a faculty and staff of thirty-two persons.

**December 15 Spectrum** makes a plea for a girl's gymnasium. It notes compulsory physical

culture class, lack of dressing rooms, and only non-prime-time hours for the basketball team to practice.

## 1904

**May 17** Bjornson monument erected on campus.

**Fall** Joining the staff this year are: Alfred H. Parrott, mathematics (later registrar until 1952); Archibald E. Minard, English and philosophy (later Dean of the School of Science and Literature until 1950); Irvin Smith, mathematics (later Dean of men until 1932); and O.O. Churchill, plant breeder.

**October 15 Spectrum** reports that enrollment for the Fall Quarter at one hundred and forty. The editor suggests that the opening date should be pushed back two weeks to allow for completion of farm work when it is late such as in 1904.

**Nov. 5, 7** NDAC and UND resume football rivalry; NDAC loses both games.

## 1905

**January 15 Spectrum** reports that "over fifty students are in the penmanship class making it necessary to divide the classes into two sections."

**February 24** Neva Stevens repeats as winner of the annual oratorical contest with a discourse on "Leo Tolstoy."

**April** NDAC receives $15,000 from Andrew Carnegie for a Library and lays cornerstone on June 7, 1905.

**June 7** Five people receive B.S. degrees including Robert Martinus Dolve, later Dean of Engineering.

**Fall** Pharmacy and chemistry move into the newly completed Chemistry building.

**October 15** **Spectrum** reports that a tackling dummy, "Henry L," and a bucking machine, "Willie," are new features on the athletic field. "These monsters are fed every afternoon, except Sunday, at 3:30."

**November 18** Fifteen hundred people, including a delegation of three hundred from Grand Forks, watch UND and NDAC play to 11-11 tie.

**December** Bulletin No. 67, "Paints and Paints Products," contains the first analysis of the leading brands of ready-mixed paints.

## 1906

**September** Professor Ladd erects a paint fence north of College Hall upon which he tests twenty types of paint and white lead.

## 1907

**January 15** The ill feelings between NDAC and UND result in the cancellation of all athletic events between the two institutions "on account of football difficulties."

**February** **Spectrum** reports on the reasons or motives for attending college: "1) Parents sent them, 2) Desire for influence, 3) Desire for life of ease and pleasure, 4) Desire for acquiring wealth, 5) Desire for

culture and love of work, 6) To study football."

**March** The new Engineering building is to be located just east of the old one and will be connected by a passage. The cost will be $95,000.

**Spring** The **Aggasiz,** the first yearbook, is issued.

**October 1** Faculty assign seating for convocations as follows: 1) Seniors, 2) Juniors, 3) Sophomores, 4) Freshmen, 5) Others. The Seniors, seated in the front rows, "will furnish a shining example to the long suffering underclassmen" who "will therefore be inspired with a determination to go and do likewise."

## 1908

**May 29** Faculty decree that there will be no more class fights.

**September 21** President Worst explains new rules to students. One rule requires that a student be reinstated each time a class is missed by acquiring a yellow card from the registrar.

**October 2** The football team chooses Leo Nemzek, star fullback from the two previous years, its captain. The coach announced that the only acceptable languages on the field are English and football; all other languages, incuding German and profanity, are prohibited. The team will have many injuries and will lose most games, including the Fargo College game, 6-23.

**October 7** Persons unknown between 8 and 9 p.m. painted all the hitching posts green and yellow. **Spectrum** reports the posts are "the shades that deck our prairies." They are "without doubt the most conspicuous objects upon the campus and as patriotic works of art didn't look half bad."

**October 13** The Engineering Department chooses the anvil and plow to symbolize the mechanical arts and agriculture in design submitted for a new seal.

## 1910

**February 22** Athletic relations between UND and NDAC resume with a basketball game before the largest crowd "ever to witness the game in Fargo." NDAC wins the game when "Peewee" Darrow, a guard, makes shot from corner, lifting his team to a 20-18 victory.

**Spring** The **Agassiz** is dedicated to the dandelion, "that sturdy little plant of unscented beauty which has. . .so valiantly upheld the colors of old A.C. on the college campus against the attacks of selfish science."

**November 21** Menu (according to **Spectrum**) for the week: Monday, Breakfast: cream of wheat with thinned milk, biscuit a la sodo, syrum served hot, postum (cold); Dinner: boiled potatoes, lamb bones with gravy, bread, biscuit (left over from preceding meal) with cottage cheese; Supper: Review of Reviews, or that which is left over from preceding meals,

Prunes. Tuesday, ditto, Wednesday, ditto, Thursday, ditto, Friday, ditto, Saturday, Grand Review.

## 1911

**February 7** Faculty decide that women should have the same physical training activities (three years) as men. They also accord credit for work in music, including individual lessons.

**February 22** National Non-Partisan League holds its presidential convention at NDAC, nominating Champ Clark for President. Booker T. Washington, Jane Adams, and Carrie Nation are among those nominated. Jane Adams receives the entire suffragette vote.

**Fall** Registration indicates a college enrollment of 149, high school, 130, and 43 in special courses. Twenty-two turn out for the first band practice while 80 men try out for the Crack Squad.

## 1912

**Fall** Copper Kettle Inn, on the corner of 10th Avenue and College Street, adds a new basement dining room where it offers regular meals at $4.00 per week.

**Fall** Football rule changes this year include 1) four downs for ten yards, 2) field reduced to one hundred yards, 3) ten-yard zone back of goal posts for forward pass, 4) onside kick eliminated, 5) one coach on the side lines. Dacotah Field is christened by a victory over the Wahpeton Indians, 112-0. In the all-important game against UND, NDAC loses 3-0.

## 1913

**February 10-14** Student Life Special train, operated and financed by students, tours state, making thirty stops. Delegation consists of representatives from all the student organizations, college orchestra, Cadet Band, Crack Squad, dramatic club, A.G. Arvold, and President and Mrs. Worst. Its purpose is to give the people of the state an impression of what the institution stands for. Approximately seventy students tour at a cost of $1,828.27.

**Spring** The Library reports that it now has accessioned 23,900 volumes, including 590 this year.

## 1914

**Fall** Faculty decree that college students may have one unexcused absence before they must appear before either the President or the Committee on Discipline.

**Fall Spectrum** warns freshmen students that they are required to wear identifiable tags: men are to wear green caps, women green ribbons in their hair.

**October 30** Thirty-one Fargo firms close for the Fargo College-NDAC football game. Over 2,000 spectators witness it. Game ends when Fargo College forfeited in a dispute over the referee's granting permission for an NDAC player to re-enter the game despite rules to the contrary. Score at the time was 7-7.

## 1915

**Winter** Winter Quarter enrollment at the various institutions in the area are: NDAC 1,311, Fargo College 552, Concordia College 357, Moorhead State Normal 1,039, Dakota Conservatory 587, Aaker's Business College 276, Dakota Business College 775, Oak Grove Seminary 105, Sacred Heart Seminary 320, Total 5,322.

**March 12** University of Southern California debate team travels to Fargo to meet with NDAC's debate team; NDAC wins.

## 1916

**Winter Qtr** NDAC students campaign to raise funds to build a YMCA building. Students and faculty raise $18,000, the city of Fargo donates $22,000 grant from the Rockefeller Institute. (The building was completed in 1920, but destroyed in 1957 by a tornado.)

**February 21** With about eight hundred attending, students hold a meeting to discuss the firing of President Worst. First item of business is to exclude the faculty from the meeting. The students write a lengthy resolution to indicate their support of Worst and his policies.

**March 8** NDAC sets record by winning eighteen straight basketball games. The team defeats UND 26-22 and wins the state championship. Bruce McKee is captain and "Dutch" Hauser is high scorer with ninety-six baskets for the year.

## 1917

**February 14** The coed edition of the **Spectrum** notes that beginning July 1, 1917, women will have the right to vote and that will bring "the first touch of democracy to North Dakota."

**May 16** Twelve NDAC men report to the camp at Fort Snelling to train for the war efforts. **Spectrum** suspends publication because several of its staff are in training.

**November 14** Professor F.W. Christianson has five hundred rats in the Chemistry building where he is conducting a test on the food value of heated and cold milk.

## 1918

**January 9** H.E. Metcalf, Biology Department, is called to the Aviation Service, the first from the faculty to be called to the military. One hundred twenty-five students are serving in the military.

**November 11** News of Armistice Day reaches the campus at 2:30 a.m. About 8 a.m. the town and the campus begin celebrating with flags on buildings and cars. Classes start but they let out early.

**December 2** First issue of the revived **Spectrum** published. Ethel Tousley, Editor-in-Chief, asks for help in the editorial "Are we or are we Not to Have a **Spectrum** This Year?"

**December 2** Ten of the men attending the Agricultural Vocational School died within the past three weeks of pneumonia following influenza.

## 1919

**May 2** Arbor Day is celebrated by planting memorial trees on campus in commemoration of the death in the war of men from NDAC. President Ladd states that one tree, at the gate of the campus, will honor Lt. Mark Heller. Twelve men were honored.

**October 2** The Student Commission discusses the question of a name change for the institution, the present name, NDAC, suggesting that agriculture is the only subject taught here.

**December 2** Stock-judging team places high in Chicago contest: third in cattle, fourth in hogs, and ninth in horses. George Hanson wins trophy as premier judge over ninety college men.

## 1920

**January 12** Students overwhelmingly favor the adoption of the Peace Treaty and League of Nations, 185-34. The faculty also favors adoption, 50-5.

**March 8** Jeanette Rankin, the first Congresswoman, speaks at convocation on the International Conference of Women held in Switzerland. Its key issue was the ways and means to alleviate the famine conditions in Europe.

**March 11** Phi Upsilon Omicron Sorority purchases a house on Twelfth Avenue and Fifteenth Street.

# The
# Early
# Years

*1890-1920*

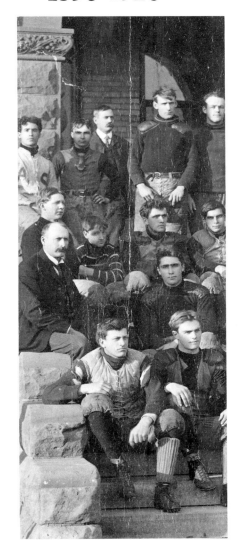

*"Picture in your mind's eye a field of golden wheat in Section 36, Fargo Township, with no buildings to mar its botanical beauty. When the train arrived in Fargo, railway freight cars lying on their sides as a result of a recent tornado and Indian braves in feathered full-dress regalia sitting near the depot were his first impressions. Immediately his thoughts returned to the letter recently received from his mother in Michigan warning him not to go to that 'awful' place of Fargo, with its dangerous tornadoes and the possibility of getting 'scalped' by Indians. He bravely continued on his way, although with some anxiety, to begin a new job in this 'frontier' country."*

This describes C.B. Waldron's initial encounter with Fargo when he arrived in July 1890, the first and only member of the staff at the College or the Experiment Station. He was twenty-four.

Despite Waldron's early impulse to flee the territory, he remained in the employment of the institution for fifty years, from 1890 until his retirement in 1940. He would occupy several positions including botanist, horticulturalist, and Dean of Agriculture.

Stockbridge

## Enter Horace Stockbridge, chemist for the Imperial Court of Japan, and a cast of thousands

Fargo College, a Congregational college located just south of Island Park, provided space for NDAC classes until a building could be constructed. Thirty students attended the first class, a special winter short course for farmers in January 1891.

Horace Edward Stockbridge, 33, hired by the Board of Trustees as President and Director of the Experiment Station, remained for only five years as head of the institution. Many of his appointments would stay long after his departure: Henry Luke Bolley, 24, biologist, 1890-1946; Edwin F. Ladd, 33, chemist (and later College President and United States Senator), 1890-1921; Harry W. McArdle, 24, mathematician and business manager, 1891-1933. Lois Hooper served as the President's secretary until she became Mrs. C.B. Waldron.

Bolley

Ladd

McArdle

Hooper

In January 1892 students and faculty moved to their new home, College Hall, later named Old Main. The building stood on a bare prairie of dust, devoid of surrounding trees and shrubbery. Planting the first tree, a major event, encouraged the participants to pose for a picture. Reports say that Professor McArdle spent much of his first two or three years planting trees.

Jessamine Slaughter, the first woman to enroll for the regular college term in September 1891, reported, "One afternoon they took me in their horse and buggy to see the Main Building, then under construction. It was way out of town and the only building on a plowed section, a lonely sight on a level prairie."

Francis Hall, built in 1893 at a cost of $17,000 from bricks fired in Fargo, was named in honor of the first president of the Board of Trustees. The first floor, used for domestic economy classes, also housed women students and some faculty. The second floor had rooms for about fifty men. Shown here is a "typical" men's room belonging to Robert B. Reed and Ralph D. Ward, two of the first five to graduate from the institution June 25, 1895. Later the Extension Service, and ultimately the College of Pharmacy, used Francis Hall for their offices.

## An engineer and a few sets of tools

When Edward S. Keene was hired in 1892 as professor of engineering he arrived to find a department which consisted of a few sets of tools. The next year the Legislature appropriated money for a mechanical building (now South Engineering) which provided classrooms, offices, laboratories, and a large hall on the second floor. Believing that most students did not have the background for technical engineering, Keene started practical courses, like blacksmithing, that students could handle. Later architecture was added. Professor Keene, who subsequently became Dean, remained at the institution until 1928.

## John Shepperd, agriculturist

John H. Shepperd was appointed professor of agriculture and agriculturalist at the Field Station in 1893. He quickly won international prizes for both plant and animal breeding. Shepperd saved the fortunes of farmers in the western part of the state when he convinced them to give up dryland farming and pursue more profitable dairying and ranching, suited to the land. He supervised the collegiate livestock judging at the Chicago International Livestock Show for twenty-seven years, a competition emulated today by the NDSU Little International in Shepperd Arena.

**"Why didn't we go for something big?"**

Fargo and NDAC never experienced severe town-gown problems. Some city residents had wished that they had obtained "something big" from the territorial government, and occasionally students exerting the exuberance of youth exceeded the boundary of good manners and irritated the city residents. Basically, however, the well-being of one meant the well-being of the other and one's tragedies affected the other. This is Fargo prior to June 7, 1893, looking north on Broadway from Second Avenue.

Fargo downtown following the fire of June 7, 1893, including a view looking south between Broadway and Roberts Street from 4th Avenue.

## Bolley and the Aggies outmaneuver the Sioux

The "Aggies" played their first football game in the fall of 1894 against the University of North Dakota. They won both their first and second games. Short of men, UND used its military instructor and NDAC put in Professor T.D. Hinebauch, then thirty-four years old. Luke Bolley, a former quarterback at Purdue, was the coach.

## Begin the music!

Other student activities included the Mandolin Club that apparently admitted students from the preparatory school, military training, and the Cadet Band.

## The President is a communicator

John Henry Worst, named President in 1895, became known as the "Father of the North Dakota Agricultural College," holding the office for twenty-one years. Although clearly a political appointment, he proved a competent administrator who retained the able men already at the institution and appointed additional good people. Worst's special contribution was his ability to communicate with the farmers of the state and win at least partial acceptance for the farm scientists.

*"There are those who, taking advantage of the name 'agricultural college,' would limit its mission to teaching subjects relating exclusively to technical activities on the farm. The purpose of the land-grant institution is to afford 'liberal and practical education for the industrial classes in the several pursuits and professions of life.'*

*In conformity with law and the general welfare, the curricula of these colleges emphasize such sciences and culture subjects as seem necessary to place the productive man, be he farmer or engineer, on the same intellectual plane as the business or professional man."* - President Worst's mission statement.

The campus about 1900. The *Prospectus* of 1891 stated: *"It is intended that the curriculum of the institution shall supplement the public school system of the state and that its course of study shall begin where the best common schools of the state leave off. . .The advantages of the institution are therefore open to all citizens of the state of either sex over the age of fifteen years, who shall satisfy the faculty of the college. . .Tuition is free to all the students admitted to the regular course. Furnished rooms cost from $3 to $8 per month."*

## A very good buy

Built in 1897 at a cost of $1,500, the Armory, later renamed Festival Hall, was used as a drill hall for military training, banquets, dances, and physical education. It would be heavily used as an all-purpose auditorium for the next 85 years.

In 1898 the *Spectrum* reported: *"Some four years ago, there was introduced to the athletes of this school an invigorating, enthusiasm-creating game known as football—now a new child presents himself, but how different he is from his brother who came in his canvas suit, heavy spiked shoes and with hair that would put to shame a cap sheaf on North Dakota wheat shock. This new child basketball, has found a warm reception. . .even our sisters are falling in love with him."*

# Half-century recruits

C.S. "Doc" Putnam began a colorful career at NDAC in 1903 where he remained, with a brief exception, until his death in 1944. Trained as a medical doctor, he was hired to teach arithmetic, hygiene, and sanitary science by the institution after his Fargo office burned in a fire in 1903. He did not return to medicine but instead turned eventually to music.

Lawrence Root Waldron, a younger brother of "C.B.," graduated from NDAC in 1899. Leaving NDAC in 1905 to become superintendent of the Dickinson Branch Station, he returned in 1916 and remained until his retirement in 1952. He specialized in plant breeding. Waldron's rust-resistant strains of wheat added millions to the nation's agricultural economy.

Alfred H. Parrott, employed in 1904 to teach mathematics, two years later became registrar where he served, with brief exceptions, until 1952. He was one of the prime movers behind the founding of the American Association of Registrars and Admission Officers. Upon his retirement he was elected executive secretary of the NDAC Alumni. He married one of his students, Pearl Canniff, in 1908.

Archibald E. Minard, another member of the 1904 class, was hired to teach English and philosophy, later becoming Dean of the School of Science and Literature in 1919. In 1908 the *Spectrum* accused him of "stealing one of the girls from the Sophomore class" for a bride. After working one summer in the Dakota wheat fields, he wrote the words for the college hymn, "The Yellow and the Green." Doc Putnam collaborated with the music. Minard retired in 1950.

## Room to grow

As early as 1898 the *Spectrum* complained about the "overcrowded conditions of our classrooms." In 1901 the Legislature responded by building the first section (now the south third of the building) of the Science Hall, adding the central portion in 1919. In 1951 the building was renamed Minard Hall, in honor of Dean Minard.

## "Suck up your gut!" Major Ulio and the Crack Squads

The terms of the Morrill Act and state law both required military training. For a period in the early years the College could not locate an instructor or secure equipment. In 1897 the U.S. War Department began to supply both. Captain James Ulio was assigned in 1901 and remained a decade. He organized weekly parades that became "a feature of college life attended by crowds which thronged the balconies of the armory," where cadets practiced. Out of this grew the "Crack Squad" which consisted of eight selected men for exhibition drill.

## Shhh, shush. . .Mrs. McVeety is watching

The first library was a room in Old Main and the President's secretary also served as the librarian. Following President Worst's three years of corresponding with Andrew Carnegie's secretary, the renowned philanthropist contributed $18,400 toward the construction of the Library, later renamed Putnam Hall. It was dedicated in 1906 when the institution's 8,000 volumes were transferred. Ethel McVeety became the first head librarian, remaining at that position until she retired June 1944. William Hunter states that "To thousands of students Mrs. McVeety was identified with the library; they remember her 'Sh-Shushing' their frequent attempts just to visit."

The Library, which grew quickly, contained 30,455 volumes in 1920. By the end of the decade it had become apparent that an addition was necessary. Although the Legislature approved the addition, Governor Schafer vetoed it. During the 1930s the College attempted to obtain a new Library through WPA funds. President Eversull noted, "the library seating capacity is about 75. It should be 400."

## A spectacular fire in chemistry

A panoramic view of the campus includes the Library (Putnam), first part of Science Hall (Minard), Chemistry building, and College Hall with students in the center. The Chemistry building was constructed in 1905. A spectacular fire destroyed the building, a greenhouse, and a power plant and threatened the remainder of the campus on December 24, 1909. Losses, listed at $85,000 were insured for about $40,000.

Chemistry would remain an important part of the curriculum. When the Chemistry building burned, the College immediately started plans for a new one.

# New recruits, '07-9

Arvold

Weeks

Slocum

Sudro

Stevens

Dolve

Alfred G. Arvold was appointed to the English and Speech Department in 1907. Later he became head of the Public Speaking Department. As founder of the Little Country Theater, he had an inclination for producing spectacular shows. He remained at the institution until 1952.

A.D. Weeks, a former English professor at Valley City, was named English professor in 1907. In 1917 he became Dean of the newly created School of Education, remaining at the college for the next two decades.

R.H. Slocum, another member of the class of 1907 when he became professor of civil engineering, was primarily concerned with teaching and the faculty. Twice, in 1917 and 1923, he served on committees to revise the *Blue Book,* a code of rules for governing of the College. He remained at the institution until 1952.

William F. Sudro was appointed instructor in pharmacy in 1908 when pharmacy was made a department. He became head of the School of Pharmacy in 1919 and, subsequently, Dean when the school became a college.

Robert M. Dolve was selected as an assistant in agricultural engineering in 1908. In 1928 he became Dean of the School of Engineering, staying at the institution until 1954.

Orin A. Stevens, appointed assistant professor of botany in 1909, specialized in seed analysis but he also studied birds, insects, flowers, and weeds. He retired in 1956 but continued researching and writing for many more years.

## In with the new

The old Engineering building, built in 1892, was replaced with the "new" Engineering building in 1907 at a cost of $95,000. Upon its opening in October 1907, the *Spectrum* reported that it was "the most handsome and imposing building on campus," well-lighted with a large number of windows, well-heated by steam heat, and well-ventilated by a forced-air system.

## Ceres Hall—"best dorm in the state"

Ceres Hall, available for limited use in the fall of 1909, formally opened in February 1911. The *Spectrum* called it "the best dormitory in the state." Built at a cost of $105,000, it served primarily as a women's dormitory but it also contained a gymnasium, the Home Economics Department, and a dining room.

The Dining Room, located in the east wing of the first floor of Ceres Hall, had a capacity of 300.

*Menu (according to* **Spectrum***) for the week: Monday, Breakfast: cream of wheat with thinned milk, biscuit a la sodo, syrum served hot, postum (cold); Dinner: boiled potatoes, lamb bones with gravy, bread, biscuit (left over from preceding meal) with cottage cheese; Supper: Review of Reviews, or that which is left over from preceeding meals, Prunes. Tuesday, ditto, Wednesday, ditto, Thursday, ditto, Friday, ditto, Saturday, Grand Review.*

Domestic Science, later called Home Economics, included textiles and clothing courses as well as food and nutrition. At top left is a Home Economics demonstration team illustrating properly prepared food and highlighting potato cookery and North Dakota products. The below right was entitled "Ready to Serve a Country Dinner."

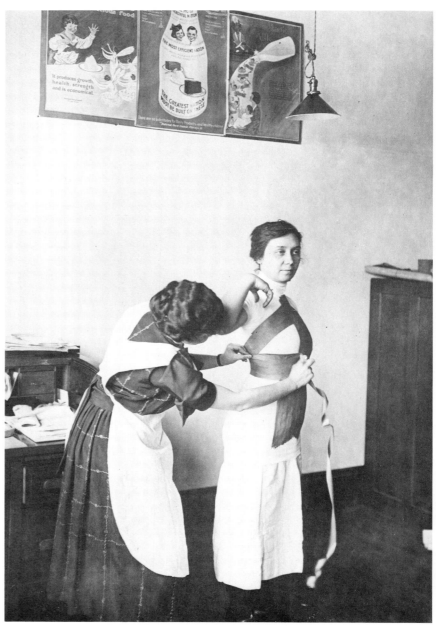

## 1909

Ceres Hall also contained dormitory rooms for women. One picture, posed for promotional purposes, illustrates the "typical room for two students." Ceres also contained a 42- by 62-foot gymnasium on the fourth floor for aesthetic dancing, but note the basketball hoop and the low ceiling.

**October 19** *Rules are published in the* **Spectrum** *governing the young ladies' dormitory:*

*1. All young ladies must be in their room after 7:30 p.m. during the school week.*

*2. All lights must be out after 10:30 p.m., and girls temporarily leaving their rooms must be careful to turn lights off. Extra charges will be incurred for violation of this rule.*

*3. Morning bells will be rung as follows: Rising. . .6:30, Breakfast. . .7:15. Dining room doors will be closed at 7:20 a.m.*

*4. Gentlemen callers will not be allowed except on Friday and Saturday evenings and may be received only in the parlors. They may not remain later than 10 p.m.*

*5. Girls are prohibited from going out after 7:30 p.m. without written permission. . . and under no circumstances to remain out later than the time indicated in such permission.*

*6. Young ladies are permitted to attend church, Y.W.C.A. meetings and regular college functions. . .but must report their intentions to the matron before going.*

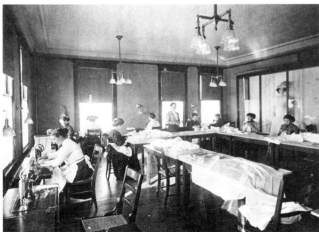

## The social graces

In 1911 the highlight of the NDAC social season was the Co-ed Prom. Students danced to such popular favorites as "I Wonder Who's Kissing Her Now" and "They Get Dippy When I Do That Two-step Dance."

## Ladd and the chemists — making paint stick

By spring 1912, the new Chemistry building (later renamed Ladd Hall) was completed under the direction of Professor Ladd. Below is a section of the experimental paint, oil, varnish, and dry-color plant. The equipment included stone mills, a mixer, an oil press, a filter press, and several precipitation tanks. Students extracted oil from flaxseed and made paints, varnishes, and dry color in this laboratory.

Professor Ladd specialized in the chemistry of foods, paints, linseed oil, and cereal chemistry. He discovered some paints contained a high percentage of water, sometimes fish oil or petroleum instead of linseed oil, and clay rather than white lead. His research and accompanying publicity began a love-hate relation with industry. At the same time, industry recognized the value of the research and began to come to NDAC for graduates in the field. (The paint fences used by the department to test the lasting qualities are also pictured here.)

## The dairymen

The Department of Dairying was popular, particularly during the early years. Headed by E.E. Kaufman, it worked closely with the Farmers' Institutes conducting meetings throughout the state; in 1901-1902 nearly 10,000 people attended the programs.

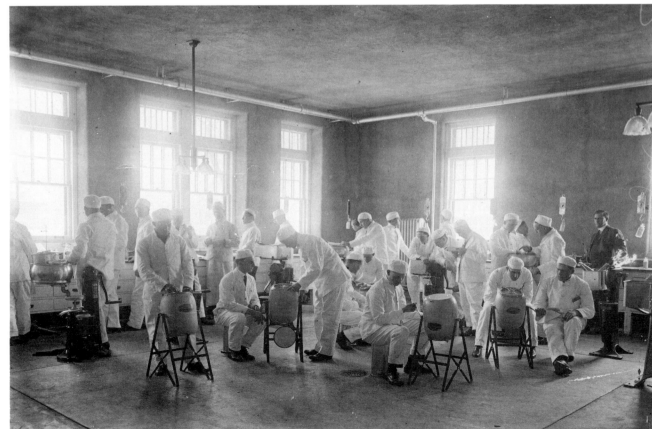

## Van Es and the vets

Leunis Van Es, appointed to the chair of veterinary science in 1902, continued in that position for eighteen years. He did much research in the various diseases of livestock, including hog cholera and avian tuberculosis. After resigning in 1920, he headed the Department of Pathology and Hygiene at the University of Nebraska. In recognition of his work, NDAC named the Veterinary Science building for him and awarded him an honorary doctorate in 1946.

## Life of an Englishman

Doc Putnam must have summoned all his contacts in the NDAC community for this impressive cast to extoll the life of an Englishman in the Gilbert and Sullivan operetta *HMS Pinafore*.

## The Little Country Theater—first act

The Little Country Theatre, Professor Arvold's idea, formally opened February 10, 1914, with the play "Miss Civilization." When Arvold discovered that NDAC had no proper stage and that no one used the chapel in Old Main, he saw possibilities in the small space for a stage. He built one that gave the illusion that it was larger and bought seating for about two hundred. To encourage the theater in small towns, he had a circulating play library.

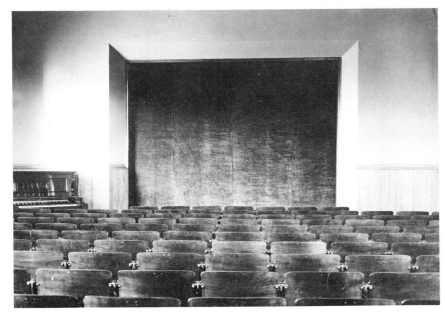

## Basketweavers and blacksmiths

Students also could gain practical experience in varied areas, from basketweaving to blacksmithing. Note sign in the forge area: "Do Not Talk to Students."

## Worst fired; Ladd hired

On February 19, 1916, when the Board discharged President Worst, students rallied to his cause and issued a resolution supporting the President and his policies. Students, faculty, and state reactions, however, were diffused when the Board nominated Professor Edwin Ladd as acting President. Ladd, a respected professor, was well known in the state and country for his emphasis and support for pure-food legislation, investigation of the milling and baking qualities of durum wheat, and his paint investigations. Although the Board meant the selection of Ladd to be temporary, Ladd experienced a loss of memory on that point and the Board did not think it would be politically expedient to remove another President.

## Science Hall enlarged

Science Hall was enlarged in
1918 so that classes like this
zoology laboratory would not be
so crowded.

## The Pharmics find a home

Francis Hall first served as a dormitory, then as offices for the Extension Service, and finally as space for Pharmacy. To the left, pharmacy students are receiving practical experience in working in the Dispensary of the Pharmacy Laboratory under the watchful eyes of Professor Sudro.

## The AC prepares for war

The ROTC Cadet Officers under
the command of Lt. Herron
about 1914.

## The AC goes to war

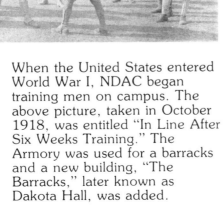

When the United States entered World War I, NDAC began training men on campus. The above picture, taken in October 1918, was entitled "In Line After Six Weeks Training." The Armory was used for a barracks and a new building, "The Barracks," later known as Dakota Hall, was added.

Ceres Hall Dining Room served as their mess hall while the men received instruction in such varied activities as boxing, telegraphing, and preparing for inspection.

News of the Armistice reached the town and campus about 2:30 a.m. and by 3:00 a.m. the whole town and campus were celebrating. Following the war the campus could return to normal and such practices as Gay Cat Day returned.

## Life returns to normal

Women took charge of the campus during the war, and for a time afterward, the ratio of women to men was about 1:1. Gradually, male students began returning to campus in greater numbers, and the old ratio of far more men to women, common in technical and professional schools, became the norm for another 50 years.

The car—that rare item
everyone wanted and nobody
had. There must have been
some wistful looks in the
direction of this roadster as
students hopped aboard the next
best thing, the streetcar bound
for downtown.

## End of an era

The era came to an end with the commencement of 1920, President Ladd's last one. Endorsed by the Non-Partisan League, Ladd won the nomination and was elected to the United States Senate. Friendly and a gracious host, he held receptions for both the faculty and the student body; Ladd's wife became accustomed to serving additional guests that he might bring home. As a chief administrative officer, however, he was frequently dogmatic and arbitrary, attempting to enforce his sometimes puritanical views on the students, including a dictum of no smoking. He served the College well, but it was soon to enter a new and faster era.

# The Best and Worst of Times

Charles Dickens wrote of another era but with words that correctly describe the period:

"It was the best of times, it was the worst of times, it was the age of wisdom, it was the age of foolishness, it was the epoch of belief, it was the epoch of incredibility, it was the season of light, it was the season of darkness, it was the spring of hope, it was the winter of despair."

NDAC had five presidents during this age, each giving the institution a certain direction, but all influenced by the seasons.

John Coulter's era, 1921-1929, epitomized good times, or the "spring of hope." With the war over and with a somewhat stern, puritanical President on his way to Washington, prosperity, although somewhat tarnished in the agricultural Midwest, seemed possible for all.

Born in East Grand Forks and a graduate of the University of North Dakota, Coulter became a great booster of the College and the state. He sponsored a contest among students that originated the slogan "Our State is Our Campus." North Dakota, the center of North America, was another theme. He told the state that North Dakota was "the richest and most resourceful of the states."

NDAC grew from 480 students to 1,447 by 1929. The state, however, did not build any new facilities during that same period

and by the end all basement and attic rooms were being used.

Some might call the period an "age of wisdom." Professors developed new courses and new programs and the College even had its own radio station, WPAK. NDAC also took on a more organized appearance with activities grouped into schools and, within the schools, departments. After the revision of the **Blue Book,** recognized as the constitution of the College, Coulter agreed to follow it. The American Association of University Professors organized a chapter in 1927. Dean A.D. Weeks, Department of Education, began a summer school in 1921 which continued until 1933. T.W. Thordarson was employed as director of correspondence courses in 1925.

Student-faculty relations became less personal with the growth of both the student body and faculty. Orientation was initiated in order to inform the first-year students of college life and assist them in adjusting to the new surroundings. Students became more involved in other ways. They were encouraged to participate in athletics, with the institution winning conference titles in football, basketball, and cross country. The Saddle and Sirloin Club, modeled after Chicago's club, was formed in 1922 and the first Little International Livestock Show was held.

It was, of course, the roaring twenties, and an "age of foolishness." The literary societies died but fraternities and sororities were born. Gay Cat Day was inaugurated as a fun day in the spring when the yearbook, later called the **Bison,** was released. In June 1929 the era came to an end with the resignation of Coulter who accepted a position as chief economist of the U.S. Tariff Commission.

After a brief interim John H. Shepperd, who first came to the institution in 1893, was appointed Acting President, and later President, guiding the College through a period that began in a positive fashion. With the coming to power of the Republicans, the Legislature appropriated funds for NDAC to construct two desperately needed buildings, a men's residence hall and a physical education building.

The honeymoon did not last long, however, and the "season of darkness" became a time of fiscal nightmares. The 1933 Legislature reduced NDAC's appropriation by 59 percent, forcing it to slice salaries severely, reduce staff, and cut operating budgets. Besides the Legislature's setting maximum salaries at all institutions at $1,920, the governor requested all state employees to pledge five percent of their salaries to finance a political paper and proposed a two-percent sales tax on items people bought. Further complicating the fiscal chaos, the Board of Administration appointed as Secretary of the College, Steve Hagan, who had political ambitions of his own.

Some faculty believed that Shepperd should have been able to do more in obtaining higher budgets and greater economic security. Dissidents established a local of the American Federation of Teachers. Faculty also criticized a reorganization of the College units designed to reduce administrative costs.

The Shepperd era, however, did have some bright spots. Enrollments continued to grow in response to some creative efforts. To secure part-time jobs for students, the College hired an employment secretary. Bachelor kitchens were installed for men students. Agricultural research, despite financial difficulties, achieved many accomplishments, including progress in the study of emergency feeds for livestock, the breeding of better strains of grains, and in the control of insect pests and animal and plant diseases. The athletic teams established the tradition of victory, the basketball team winning two straight conference championships and the football team winning a conference championship.

Shepperd's resignation ushered in the "winter of despair," often referred to as "the Purge." When it accepted Shepperd's resignation, the Board appointed John C. West, President of the University of North Dakota, Acting President. At the same time, it sent letters of dismissal to seven of the higher-ranking members of the staff including Robert Dolve, Dean of the Engineering School; Alba Bales, Dean of the Home Economics School; A.H. Parrott, Registrar; I.W. Smith, Dean of Men and Professor of Math; P.J. Olson, Assistant Dean of the Agricultural School; N.D. Gorman, County Agent Leader; and Jean Traynor, secretary to President Shepperd. In addition, the Board relieved H.L. Walster, Dean of Agriculture, as Director of the Experiment Station and Extension Service.

The records give no clear reason for the actions. While Board members, appointed by the governor, claimed they made the changes in the best interests of the institution, most observers believed that Governor Langer sought control of the Extension Service and Experiment Station as well as the Board of Administration.

Regardless of the reasons the purge was devastating to the institution. Not only did it lose top staff people with the dismissal but several other highly respected people left including A.F. Yeager, internationally famous plant breeder, and L.M. Roderick, Professor of Animal Pathology. In the crowning blow, the North Central Association of Colleges and Secondary Schools removed NDAC from the list of accredited schools April 7, 1938.

The loss of accreditation unified faculty and students alike. Besides holding mass meetings, students staged a torchlight parade in the Fargo streets where they burned in effigy four state officials. More importantly, plans were made to propose change. With assistance from graduates and friends, the students began a campaign for passage of a constitutional amendment to establish a non-political Board of Higher Education to replace the Board of Administration. A committee of eleven, chosen from the student body to head the effort, included Reuben Arnason, Fargo; Maurice Benidt, Lidgerwood; Millard Borke, Hillsboro; John Clason, Akeley, Minnesota; Florenz Dinwoodie, Fargo; Orville Goplen, Fargo; Dale Hogoboom, Fargo; John Lynch, LaMoure; John McGregor, Page; Mercedes Morris, Wahpeton; and DeLawrence Nelson, Fargo. The **Spectrum** reported: "Members of the committee took charge of radio campaigning, newspaper publicity, club organization, naming of student county committees, addressing state groups, correspondence and general organization of the campaign. Offices were set up in the Barracks where typewriters and mimeographs were installed. Office supplies, stationery and stamped envelopes were furnished by downtown firms."

These efforts were rewarded when the voters agreed and passed the constitutional amendment June 28, 1938.

NDAC, its faculty and students, were all eventually vindicated. North Central reinstated the institution March 30, 1939, a Board of Higher Education was named, and the seven dismissed members offered re-employment.

A new President, F.L. Eversull, came to the institution September 15, 1938, to begin his term under most trying conditions. Lacking experience in the administration of an agricultural college and unfamiliar with North Dakota, he had difficulties, as an ordained minister, gaining the confidence of practical-minded farmers and businessmen. His largest asset was being a vice-president in the North Central Association.

Shortly after the purge ended a new "season of darkness" came, not only to the campus but to the entire nation, with the advent of World War II. When the College mobilized to meet the needs of a nation at war, enrollment fell but Army personnel utilized the institution's facilities. After an officers candidate school opened in 1942, with courses lasting twelve weeks, approximately 1,300 men received commissions here. Other programs included a school for Army engineers and a special unit Army Specialized Training Program.

Following World War II a whole new set of problems faced the President. The veterans felt that they were receiving an inadequate education. Although not directly blaming Eversull, several believed the President was not doing enough to correct the situation. In April 1946, various campus organizations held a meeting and passed a resolution indicating dissatisfaction. Realizing that his services now were of limited value to the institution, Eversull resigned June 11, 1946, his term of office perhaps the most tumultuous of any President's: the conclusion of the depression, the purge, World War II, and the beginning of the boom years.

John H. Longwell, appointed President to succeed Eversull July 24, 1946, came to NDAC in 1941 as a specialist in animal nutrition and breeding. Active in College affairs, he headed up a committee on curriculum and postwar planning.

With the "spring of hope," the school was bursting with energy and students. Although the "old" great professors were retiring, new youthful instructors were joining the ranks. The institution mourned the loss of those who died in the war efforts but rejoiced in the baby boom taking place in Silver City and other married-student housing.

Expressing concern for increasing the College's physical plant, Longwell and his staff pointed out that the plant, adequate for 1,400, now had 2,350 students crowded into classrooms, laboratories, and dormitories. The students, reacting more quickly than the Legislature, voted to create a Student Union Building fund in 1947; sufficient housing and classroom space had to wait for another administration.

Sports, however, did not maintain the same sense of hope and enthusiasm as the rest of the institution. Returning veterans, many of whom had participated earlier, initially showed great interest in sports. But a rapid turnover of coaches occurred, and the larger universities were more successful in recruiting athletes. During the 1947-1948 season, Bison teams finished in the North Central Conference cellar in both football and basketball.

Longwell surprised everyone when he submitted his resignation late in July 1948, stating that he wanted to return to research, the work for which he had trained.

Thus the era ended as it began, poised for a season of growth and the dream of stability.

# A Timeline: The Middle Years

## 1921

**October 21** Alpha Gamma Rho Fraternity moves into its new house on the corner of Tenth Avenue and College Street.

**November 3** Rules and regulations for social functions, as passed by the faculty, include 1) securing permission to hold parties on or off campus, 2) two chaperones in attendance who will file a report on conduct, 3) prohibition of smoking.

**December 3** Two hundred respond to the call for volunteers to prepare the grounds north of the YMCA for a skating rink. President Coulter and Professor I.W. Smith sponsor the project and are on hand to assist. The Lyceum of Engineers has charge of supplying lighting for the rink. Plans are underway to introduce hockey on the athletic program of both men and women.

## 1922

**January 20** Athletic Board recognizes hockey as a college sport. The **Spectrum** notes that no other colleges in the Northwest play hockey.

**March 2** **Spectrum** advocates changing the name of the institution. A survey indicates that most campus people favor North Dakota State College.

**March 17** The North Dakota State Club votes to change the name of the athletic team from the "Aggies" to the "Bisons".

**March 31** Architects draw up plans for a new Agriculture Building (Morrill Hall) to be constructed on the grounds now occupied by Francis Hall.

**Fall** Enrollment will pass 1,000, a twenty-four percent increase over last year. The total includes 124 high school students and 107 disabled veterans.

**October 21** The Saddle and Sirloin Club holds its first meeting. Its members, students from the School of Agriculture, will sponsor the Little International Livestock Shows.

**December 7** **Spectrum** publishes the new rules for interclass basketball games: 1) no concrete padding, 2) razors, knives, and broken glass must be left on the sidelines, 3) games will automatically stop when one side reaches 300 points, 4) swearing at opponents, when freshmen or girls are present, is barred.

## 1923

**January 2** Ten-week short course will bring an additional 150 students on campus. Course will include instruction in auto and tractor mechanics, elevator management, farm crops, farm management, and dairying.

**October 17** E.S. Keene, Dean of the School of Mechanic Arts, directs the radio broadcasting service of the college. The station broadcasts lectures and musical recitals at 7:00 p.m. each Monday, Wednesday, and Friday.

**October 31** The Lincoln Log Cabin is added to the Little Country Theatre.

**December 8** Faculty Council approves two new sororities, both organized on a social basis. Gamma Kappa Phi has ten charter members and Phi Kappa Lambda has eleven.

## 1924

**March 12** Ceres Hall nearly burns; fire is discovered in the rubbish box in the Home Economics Cooking Locker Room. Women could not leave because of locked doors and windows.

**March 13** Faculty approve one social fraternity, Alpha Sigma Tau, with eleven charter members, and two professional fraternities, Alpha Phi Omega, Chemistry, and Mu Pi, Pharmacy (later accepted as a chapter of Kappa Psi, a national pharmacy fraternity).

**November** Professor J.H. Shepperd takes his first leave of absence in thirty years, planning a vacation in the Mediterranean and study in Great Britain, France, and Denmark. Professor Shepperd will delay the trip until January so he can serve as superintendent of the judging contest at the Chicago International Livestock Show.

## 1925

**February 17** Dean H.L. Walster, School of Agriculture, announces a change in the course of study which will allow more electives; formerly 178 units in agriculture were nonelective, now it is 124.

**April 17** Cross is burned during the prom. No one knows who lit it or why, but possibly the KKK was responsible.

**May 1** Eugene Fitzgerald succeeds Edward Yocum as head of the **Spectrum.** Carrie Dolphin named first woman editor of the **Bison.**

**December 1** College post office becomes a Fargo branch office. The official address is now State College Station, Fargo, North Dakota.

## 1927

**January 21** Bison hockey team has its first home match with St. Thomas on the Island Park rink. Capt. Thomas Smith is the coach with Palmer Severtson, captain. The team splits the two-game series.

**March 14** Governor A.G. Sorlie vetoes the building appropriation bills killing the additions to the Agriculture Building and Science Hall.

**May 4** Blue Key, a national fraternity with 27 chapters, organizes with ten charter members. It departs from usual fraternity practice in that it is not secret and its primary object is that of service.

**May 19** Pi Gamma Mu, Social Science Honorary Society, is formed with 24 students, faculty and alumni installed.

**May 21** North Central Conference is restructured with six members: AC, UND, USD, SDAC, Morningside and Creighton.

## 1928

**Feb 10, 11** The Little Country Theatre presents "The Vikings of Helgeland" by Henrik Ibsen. Alfred Arvold, founder of the Little Country Theatre, is the director and Phyllis Heimark, Ruby Oscarson, and Hjalt Thorfinnson play leads.

**February 10** A survey of freshmen indicates thirty-two percent attend NDAC because of subjects taught, twenty-five percent due to location, and ten percent because of low costs.

**Summer** Four sororities acquire homes: Kappa Delta house, 1002 7th Street North, will accommodate fifteen; Sigma Theta, 1026 13th Street (founded in 1908 at Fargo College and moved to NDAC in 1922 with the closing of the College); Phi Kappa Lambda, 1108 9th Street; and Alpha Xi Beta.

## 1929

**January 29** Before a packed house, NDAC Debate Team meets a team from the University of Sydney, Australia, in the Little Country Theatre. The question is "Resolved, that scientists should take a ten-year holiday."

**March 4** With classes excused, the campus people crowd into the Little Country Theatre to hear the inaugural ceremonies in Washington, D.C., on the radio. CBS presented the program over WDAY. It came in on a Kolster radio made possible by the Stone Piano Company.

**March 22** Governor Schafer signs bills for additions to Science Building and Agriculture Building but vetoes the Powerhouse and Library addition. He also signs the bill for a new physical education building to be completed by 1931.

**May** NDAC ROTC Rifle Team wins the 1929 National Intercollegiate Indoor Rifle Matches for the second consecutive year. With First Lieut. Frank Rose as coach, the team scored 7,691 out of 8,000, a new record.

**Fall** President Coulter resigns and Dr. John Shepperd becomes Acting President.

**Fall** Attendance regulations, recently adopted, stipulate 1) a two-percent reduction in grades for any unexcused absence, 2) three unexcused absences from any class will place the student on probation, which bars the student from intercollegiate or student activities, 3) upon twenty-percent absence the student will be given a failing grade, 4) absences before and after vacations shall count as two cuts, 5) faculty will file daily attendance records with the registrar.

## 1930

**February 1** Sigma Theta will become Alpha Omicron, the 37th chapter in the National Gamma Phi Beta Sorority. Margaret Ballard is local president.

**February 18** Ground breaking will start this spring for new physical education building and men's dorm. The athletic building will have seating for 3,500 with a swimming pool included under the stage. The dorm will accommodate 200.

**September 20** Bison play first football game under the lights, defeating Concordia 6-0.

**October 14** Rules for new men's dorm include 1) guest hours from 4 to 7:30 p.m., 2) smoking in rooms but not halls, 3) no cooking in rooms.

**October 17** Mrs. Hendvit is the new manager of the Ceres Hall cafeteria which serves 450 students three meals daily for $5.00 a week per student. Twenty-six students are now working in the cafeteria.

## 1931

**May 29** Seniors exempted from the existing no-cut systems, providing they have an 85 average in the preceding term.

**October 15** New absence system replaces the old system. The new plan grants two unexcused absences for every course. A study, however, indicates that under the rigid no-cut system, averages rose one and one-half points.

**December 5** NDAC loses its first basketball game in the new physical education building to the University of Minnesota, 18-31. The team, however, will win seven consecutive conference victories and the North Central championship.

## 1932

**April 18** Salaries of all employees at NDSU suffer a ten-percent cut, saving the state $10,500.

**September 16** Fifteen hundred applications have been received for part-time jobs located by the NDSU Employment Bureau.

**Fall** The Bison football team this year will play George Washington University, Army, and Oklahoma City University. Although losing to GWU and Army, the team will have an unblemished conference record.

**October 11** The enrollment of three freshmen women in the Department of Agriculture, Ethel Tulchinsky, Flora Elliot, and Sadie Rosenberg, constitutes the largest number of women in the department at any one time.

## 1933

**Winter** Leonard Saalwaechter's basketball team wins second straight conference championship. Bob Wier, 6'7" center, Vic McKay, and Don Arthur receive All-Conference honors. Seniors and alumni beat Globetrotters 26-25.

**Fall** Women's physical education only course of study removed from curriculum due to appropriation cut; other cuts absorbed by reducing salary of college workers.

**Fall** A male student needs $176.50 for the entire year, including $87.50 for the first term (tuition $12.50, breakage $3.00, military suit $20.00, student activity $5.00, matriculation fee $10.00, room $22.00, and books $15.00).

**Fall** About eighty-five graduates from the School of Chemistry are employed by over fifty paint and varnish companies.

## 1934

**Feb 10-12** Little Country Theatre celebrates its twentieth year. A.G. Arvold, founder of the theatre, presents three plays. The Peer Gynt stained-glass window is unveiled at a midnight ceremony. Ethel Barrymore, Charles Lindbergh, Knute Rockne, Lorado Taft, Edward Everett Hale III, and Richard Ely are among the guests who have signed the guest book.

**February** Advertisers in the **Spectrum** include Roxy and State Theaters, Northern School Supply, Wimmer's Jewelry, Leeby's, Black's, Fargo Toggery, Avalon Ballroom (with music by Lem Hawkins), Knight Printing, Briggs Tobacco, W.W. Wallwork, Stevenson's, Herbst's, The Palace, and Alex Stern and Company.

**February 16** College students can apply for work on a FERA project, which pays 30 cents per hour. Work begins March 1. A payroll of $2,348.10 will be distributed.

**Fall** Ceres Hall, with a capacity of 80 women, and the Men's Resident Hall, with a capacity of 160, are full. Each floor of the Men's Hall now has a telephone.

## 1935

January Board of Administration recommends a $50 salary increase—up from $1,350 a year.

**January** Letter from James Long, a student, to North Dakota Speaker of the House ignites controversy. Long claims majority of the students oppose the idea and practice of compulsory military training. Claim is disputed, however, on campus.

**April 6** A local fraternity, Alpha Sigma Tau, becomes a Sigma Alpha Epsilon chapter. Fraternity's home is at 1025 10th Street North.

**Fall** NDAC High School, which exists primarily to enable seniors of the School of Education to gain practice and experience in teaching, enrolls fifty-three for Fall term.

**October** NDAC, under Director T.W. Thordarson, will offer a new correspondence course for those persons unable to attend high school.

## 1936

**Feb 20-21** Blue Key calls the 1936 Bison Brevities "Be Yourself." James Baccus is writing and directing the show while Bill Akeley is the manager.

**May 8 Bison** is distributed; William Murphy is editor, Warner Litten is business manager.

**Fall** Freshman chemistry uses a new plan of instruction. A student now attends two large lecture sessions, two smaller quiz sections, and one laboratory period. Five graduate assistants have been hired to conduct the lab and quiz sections.

## 1937

**January 7** Dedication of the new School of Religion Building is held. A large donation from Mr. and Mrs. S. Fred Knight made the building possible.

**January** Legislature convenes to consider funds for the biennium, consolidation of courses, and compulsory ROTC. President Shepperd has pointed out that, since 1930, fifty-seven of the vacancies on the faculty have gone unfilled. The state's Budget Board recommends less than received previously.

**May 6-8** College hosts 1,000 prep students at 30th Annual May Festival. NDAC department heads plan program of cultural and vocational contests and various educational features.

**Fall** Two hundred fifty students join the new NDAC Date Bureau. At the first all-school dance, September 23, thirty-three dates were secured according to Gorman King, bureau manager.

**October** Blue Key embarks on a number of money-raising activities to pay for the big Nickel Trophy that goes to the winner of NDAC-UND game October 31. Eighteen hundred medallions are made and sold. UND wins the game 27-0.

## 1938

**April 1 Spectrum** editorial supports project known as the Missouri River Dam and Diversion Project.

**April** Committee of Eleven forms to push for a constitutional amendment establishing a nonpolitical State Board of Higher Education to replace the Board of Administration.

**May 13** Unaccredited party held to finance efforts to pass the constitutional amendment. Dorm women are granted 2 a.m. leave.

**June 16** Governor Langer's suit to enjoin North Central from removing NDAC from accredited list is denied.

**June 18** Campaign to adopt a constitutional amendment providing for a Board of Higher Education succeeds.

**August** Dr. Frank Eversull assumes post as NDAC President. The new President, the former head of Huron College, also is a vice president of the North Central Association of Colleges.

**Fall** Enrollment declines with a loss of two hundred in the freshman class. NDAC High School is discontinued due to a lack of funds.

## 1939

**Feb 8-12** Celebration of Silver Anniversary of the Little Country Theatre. Among the plays presented is Ibsen's "Peer Gynt" starring Alfred Mason Arvold, son of the founder and director, A.G. Arvold.

**February 17 Spectrum** takes a poll on whether smoking by women is sophisticated or objectionable. Students vote in favor 11, against 30, no opinion 1,359.

**May 24** Bison football team plays the Winnipeg Blue

Bombers in an exhibition rugby game before the King and Queen of England.

## 1940

**April 4-5** Bison Brevities presents "The Blue Key Turns," written by Roy Pedersen, directed by Margaret Calhoun, with music written and arranged by Frank Scott.

## 1941

**December 5** Louis Armstrong and his band play a five-hour show at the Crystal Ballroom.

**December 8** Bill Larson and Don Jones receive Army commissions ten minutes after President Roosevelt signs the declaration of war.

## 1942

**May 8** Junior-Senior prom is informal for the first time and requires a 25-cent defense stamp with a ticket.

## 1943

**Fall** Enrollment fall quarter is 586. State Legislature reestablishes compulsory military training. Approximately 1,800 Army men are stationed on campus.

## 1944

**Fall** Committee of the post-war plans, headed by J.H. Longwell, submits reports. It considers 1) accommodations for regular students, 2) short-course curriculum for returning war workers, 3) education for veterans.

## 1945

**February 8** Orville Bloch, '42, receives Congressional Medal of Honor while fighting in Italy. Beryl Newman was the first NDAC student to receive the nation's highest decoration.

**Winter** Basketball returns to NDAC for both men and women. Men have all-civilian team and one with the military; military team can only play in town.

**Fall** NDAC registration hits 712; almost a one-hundred-percent increase over last year. Ratio of men to women is one to one; however, the senior class has 61 women and only 17 men.

**Oct 26-27** After two years of inactivity, NDAC fields a football team. Homecoming returns with a parade, floats, and a football game with UND. NDAC wins 26-7. Irene Gunvaldsen is Queen.

## 1946

**April 22-23** Bison Brevities returns with a musical, "HMS Pinafore." Merle Nott and Mary Jane Shurr have the leads.

**June 6** Dr. Frank L. Eversull resigns presidency to become chief of the colleges for the 24th United States Corps Command in Korea.

**August 15** Dr. John H. Longwell, former chief of the Division of Animal Industry and Associate Director of the Experiment Station, becomes seventh President of NDAC.

**Fall** Fifty-one persons have joined the faculty since the spring term. Fall term opening postponed from September 23 until October 7 due to a local poliomyelitis epidemic.

## 1947

**January 25** Little International resumes grain- and livestock-judging contests with added features of a coed milking contest, greased-pig contest, and a dog show.

**June 5** Students vote 821-89 in favor of building a Student Union and adding five dollars per student per term to the activity fee.

**October** Trailer City names Leon Warner as its new mayor. The census lists 394 persons living in 162 trailers.

**November 21** Bison football team shares cellar in North Central with Morningside; neither team wins a conference game. Dennis Drews receives the most valuable player award.

**November 25** Gamma Phi Beta sorority defeated ATO fraternity 13-9 in the Second Annual Bromo Bowl with Margo Brunskill and Paula Nemzek scoring touchdowns. Bill Dietz and Sid Cichy refereed and often penalized ATO for holding.

## 1948

**February 27** NDAC completes a successful hockey season with an unsuccessful trip to UND, losing 6-17.

**February 28** Bison basketball finishes with a split between UND and NDAC but the Bison end the season in the conference cellar. Red Bostrom finishes his career second high scorer in the league.

**April 2** Stan Kostka resigns. Hollingsworth, former head coach at Gustavus Adolphus, becomes new head football coach. He resigns and Howard Bliss, Valley City, is appointed.

**Summer** Campaign to raise funds for a Student Union collects $175,000, with thirty people donating $1,000 each. B.F. Meinecke heads the financial committee, A. Glen Hill is president of the Union Corporation.

**July** John H. Longwell resigns as President to accept position of Dean of Agriculture at the University of Missouri.

**August 24** Dr. Fred S. Hultz accepts the presidency of NDAC.

**October 29** Gamma Phi Sorority is constructing a house at 13th Street and 13th Avenue.

**December 3** Singer Peggy Lee on the NBC Chesterfield Supper Club toasts the recently formed Rahjahs. Lee was formerly a featured singer at the Powers Coffee Club.

**December 21** Dr. Daniel Posin, Chairman of the Physics Department, appears on the ABC "Town Meeting of the Air"; the subject is "What Should We Do To Win The Cold War?"

# The Middle Years

## 1921-1948

## The College builds

Agriculture may have lost the rights to the College mascot, but it found a home during the Coulter administration. Morrill Hall, the first building dedicated to agriculture, became the center of the school's activities. Dean C.B. Waldron acted as master of ceremonies at the laying of the cornerstone for the new building May 12, 1922. President Coulter, at the dedication in January 1923, called its construction "timely. . .in a period of depressed agricultural and business stagnation in the state."

Other building during the Coulter years included an addition to Festival Hall, the Alba Bales Home Management House and fraternity houses for Alpha Gamma Rho and Theta Chi.

## The '20s campus scene

The women of Ceres Hall had a
slightly somber look in 1929, but
the decade retained its carefree
distinction. The likes of these
hemlines would not be seen
again for more than thirty years.

## Gay Cats and good fun

Gay Cat Day was a spring ritual, the day the **Bison Annual** was issued. It was a time to dress in strange costumes (as did the Misses Ostbye and Lattimer seen here with Phillip Moe) or attend the latest Clara Bow movie.

NDAC float builders were more than equal to the task of portraying the richness of the earth in this 1925 parade entry. And Doc and the band were always ready for a parade down Broadway, this one a May Festival in 1923.

Following World War I, the trend was away from literary societies to social fraternities and sororities. The Kappa Delta sorority pledges of 1928 are shown here on the steps of the Library.

Several national honorary fraternities were also on campus, the oldest being the Alpha Zeta agricultural fraternity. Four stalwart members of Alpha Zeta posed for this oval picture in 1921.

The campus YMCA was another means of fraternizing. The memory of World War I was still fresh when these veterans and students met at the Y on Armistice Day, 1920.

## Homecoming, the rite of fall

Bunting draped from South Engineering and the rest of campus signaled Homecoming. If the University was in town for the game, the ritual became less decorous.

The UND band and ROTC cadets must have been less than enthused about the way they were represented at the Homecoming parade of 1922 by some of their, no doubt well-meaning, NDAC counterparts.

The bonfire, one of the rites of Homecoming, has ceased. Vulnerability to sabotage from enemy camps, despite the best efforts of the underclassmen to guard their pile of wood; the occasional arrest of students overzealous in their pursuit of fuel for the fire; and modern fire codes brought about the demise of the bonfire.

## Football: under the lights and on the radio

Football took on new sophistication during the 1920s and early '30s. In this October 30, 1920 game, NDAC is punting from the center of the field toward the UND goal. The AC-UND series became a matter of great importance for many. A sign in the foreground reads, "Show the world Fargo is right!"

Games were well attended with as many as 6,500 spectators at the Homecoming game with UND in 1928. Captain George "Baldy" Hays of the 1928 team demonstrates how to catch the ball.

By 1930 these rugged linemen were playing under the lights with a win over Concordia, and their first game was broadcast on the radio, a loss to Michigan State 11-9.

## Hold that pyramid!

Women's physical education and athletics had its good times and its bad times. In 1933, when the state cut appropriations, women's physical education was the only course of study removed from the curriculum; the program was restored the following year. The 1920s, however, were a time of activity. The field hockey team is shown practicing October 31, 1923, while the game with an unidentified team occurred October 27, 1922. Note that the field is located west of the Library, now Putnam Hall.

Other phy-ed activities included soccer and tumbling.

## Bison with an "s"

The transition from "Aggies" to "Bison" was not without difficulty. Apparently athletic budgets in the early 1920s did not allow for such a radical change of uniforms overnight. However, the 1924 team did play eleven games on the west coast in fifteen days, presumably as the "Bison" or perhaps "Bisons," there seems to have been some confusion about the plural form of the word for the new mascot. In 1926 the team won the conference, and in 1931 the Bison(s) played their last game in the Armory, losing to UND 24-30.

The women had a more homogeneous look to their uniforms, but intercollegiate play began to wane in favor of intramurals.

Hockey was recognized as a college sport in 1922. The 1927-1928 season included a win over UND and a loss to Augsburg, shown here.

## Agriculture on campus

Dr. H.L. Walster came to the institution in 1919 to begin a thirty-five-year career. Appointed Chairman of the Agronomy Department and Dean of Agriculture in 1924, a decade later Walster became Director of the Experiment Station and Extension Service,

thus making possible closer correlation between the educational and research aims of the college.

As dean, Walster did much to improve classroom education. A class in farm management in 1924 is shown here. As a research administrator, Walster was good at getting the best from his people.

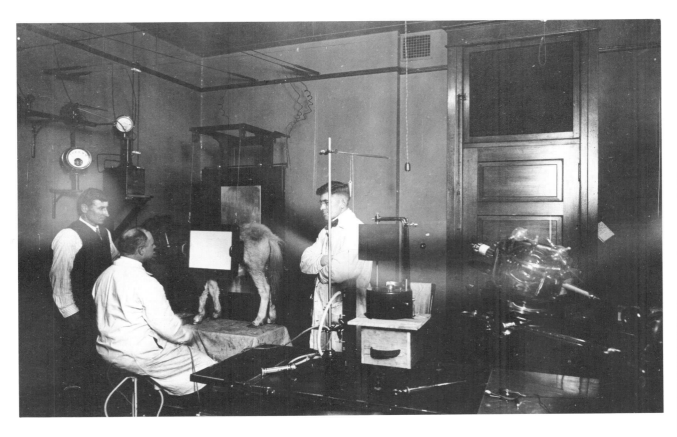

A.F. Schalk began his work in veterinary science in 1910 and remained until 1930. Schalk helped develop the Rumen fistula, a method by which a window is placed in a cow's stomach, thus making it possible to investigate digestive disturbances in ruminants.

Although located in the School of Science and Literature, bacteriology was important to agriculture. Later it was moved to the School of Agriculture for political reasons. Here a bacteriology laboratory is being conducted, December 1922. Note the number of women, which would have been unusual in the School of Agriculture.

C.I. Nelson came to NDAC in 1914, remaining until 1954. As a bacteriologist he conducted numerous experiments in flax wilt resistance and the treatment of sewage. He actively promoted student health and the Student Health Center was later named for him.

## Home Economics:
## Action and decorum

The home economists took to the field with an active extension program, just as the agriculturalists did. This canning demonstration drew an audience of whole families.

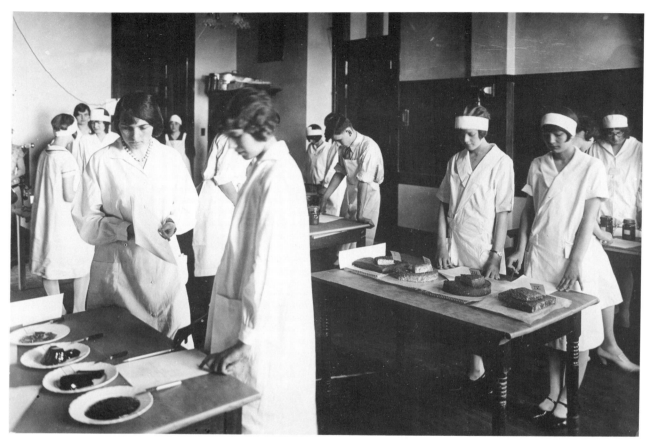

Home Economics was offered as early as 1893. Under President Coulter's organization, the school had four departments: Food and Nutrition, Clothing and Textiles, Applied Arts, and Household and Institutional Management. A foods and nutrition class with a lone male student is illustrated here.

Alba Bales, who served NDAC from 1920 to 1942, became Dean in 1936. Under her leadership the school grew from sixty students in 1920 to 316 in 1942. She became the first within the College to undertake off-campus teacher training and established the Home Management House for senior students.

This 1922 Demonstration Team from Barnes County shows off some of the youth work supervised by NDAC extension home economists. On campus, clothing and textiles students learned to judge the quality of a child's wardrobe.

This 1921 "life drawing" class for a mixed audience of architects and home ecs included a more than properly clothed model.

Ceramics was popular in the 1920s, indicated by Mary Elizabeth Pollock as she works on a clay model. The Art Studio, located in the YMCA, also doubled as a place for special parties.

## The engineers and the mechanic arts

The technical world changed after World War I, and NDAC engineering changed with it. Engineering was still known as the School of Mechanic Arts, and this broom-testing machine designed for home economics reflected the school's practical bent.

## X-rays, moving pictures and the voice-activated stoplight

In 1921 Harry Rush was hired to teach electrical engineering.

Although Dean Keene was in charge of mechanical engineering, he was also extremely interested in the applications of electronics. He brought the first moving picture projector into the state and was the first to use an x-ray machine successfully in the Northwest. In 1924 Keene and his students established WPAK, the college radio station. (WDAY took over college broadcasts in 1926.) In 1928 Edward Keene was named dean emeritus and Robert Dolve took over as dean of the school. Dolve, already a longtime member of the faculty, continued at NDAC until 1954.

In 1929, just after his appointment as dean, Dolve and some of his faculty posed with this innovation in transportation engineering, a stoplight activated by the honk of an automobile horn. Reports of how the machine fared in the field are not known. Automobiles such as this Essex were still evolving and this automobile lab was heavily used. The more traditional aspects of steam-powered systems were studied in old South Engineering.

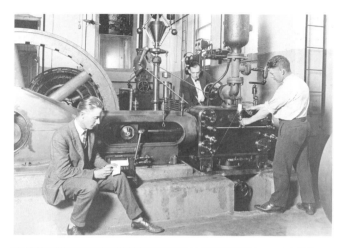

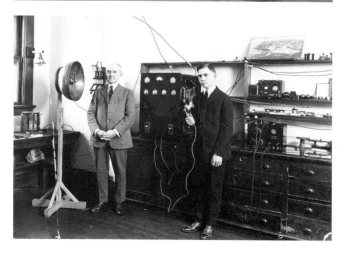

## Pressure and stress, civil engineering and physics

A testing lab supervised by Professor Bovely dealt with the problems of minute stress and large scale problems for the block and tackle. In 1924 Charles Swisher joined the faculty as head of physics, at that time a department in Mechanic Arts. These three students, with Swisher in the center, performed a pressure experiment in 1926.

## Chemistry, up from the basement

When President Ladd reorganized NDAC in 1916, chemistry became a school, a significant step up from its beginnings in the basement in Old Main. L.L. Carrick, the fellow with the jacket and bowtie in the left middle ground of this photograph, arrived at the College in 1920 and became dean in 1937 where he served until 1943. During the 1930s the Board of Administration attempted to reorganize the College and combined chemistry with engineering. Chemistry was liberated to its former status four years later.

## Pharmacy: for chills, fevers, and kindred ills

In 1901, after receiving authorization to give classes in pharmacy, NDAC outlined two- and four-year courses. Seven years later pharmacy became a division within the Chemistry Department and in 1919 a separate school was established. William F. Sudro, who came to the College in 1908 and remained for nearly fifty years, is pictured (standing lower right) with a group of students, 1930.

A Mentholatum display and a copy of the Ten Commandments were all that adorned this pharmacy lecture hall in 1930. The practice pharmacy simulated an actual drug store, minus the soda fountain.

## "The wildlife of your state"

This photograph of biologist George Miller with an owl was used in promotional literature for recruiting NDAC students. The caption read, "Learn about the wildlife of your state at NDAC." Monkeys and alligators were an added inducement.

The five mounted cranes were perhaps part of the museum established at NDAC by the U.S. Zoological Survey in the early part of the century. The project involved collecting as many known animal species as possible in each state, mounting them as taxidermy, and depositing the finds in reliable institutions. The collection is still housed at NDSU in Stevens Hall.

## John Shepperd and difficult times, 1929-1937

President Coulter resigned his office effective August 31, 1929. John Shepperd, shown here standing on the right at the Farm House with some of the students and staff, was appointed Acting President.

*My skill is still at your command,*
*My hand for friends to seek.*
—Haile Chisholm upon his
retirement.

## Casey Finnegan and those beautiful fall days

Charles "Casey" Finnegan replaced Ion Cortright as sports director July 1, 1928. Together with Presidents Coulter and Shepperd, Finnegan planned renewed activities in both intramural and intercollegiate athletics. By 1932 the football team had an unblemished conference record including a win over UND during Homecoming. The only losses in 1932 came at the hands of Army and George Washington University.

The team is shown here on an eastern road trip. These "four horsemen" from the conference champions of 1938 included number 41, All-American Ernie Wheeler. Wheeler starred in the North-South all-star game and went on to a successful professional career.

A joyous **Spectrum** announced February 18, 1930, the forthcoming construction of two badly needed buildings, a boy's dorm and a field house. The dorm, later named for O.O. Churchill, agronomist and faculty representative to the North Central Conference Athletic Board, housed 200 residents. The field house had seating for 3,500. The basement, the "pit," also served as a men's dormitory.

The fortunes of the men's basketball team improved in the 1930s. Leonard Saalwaechter's team won its second straight conference title in 1933, and Coach Bob Lowe continued the Bison on their winning ways through 1947.

Finnegan wrote in the **Spectrum** about the increased emphasis on physical training and exercise which was "in line with the changing times everywhere." The intramural program included basketball, hockey, wrestling, tumbling, and boxing. Boxing was expecially popular, drawing large crowds as in this match in Festival Hall, April 3, 1931.

## They Are The Targets In Wholesale NDAC Firing Campaign Announced Saturday---
Biographies On Page 2

Dean R. M. Dolve    Dean I. W. Smith    A. H. Parrott    Dean H. L. Walster    Dr. J. H. Shepperd    Dean Alba Bales    P. J. Olson    N. D. Gorman

Morning Edition

# THE FARGO FORUM
AND DAILY TRIBUNE

Morning Edition

VOL. 30, NO. 28          1          FARGO, N. D., SUNDAY MORNING, AUGUST 1, 1937          Twenty-two Pages          PRICE FIVE CENTS

# 7 OUT AS NDAC 'PURGE' BEGINS

The years 1937-1938, sometimes called the "purge years," were the most tragic for NDAC, but they were years in the making.

In the 1930s farmers looked to the College for help during economic depression. The governor (William Langer) and the Legislature eyed the Experiment Station and Extension Service budgets. The federal payrolls and relief funds they administered represented great potential for a political pork barrel.

Langer was convicted and removed from office in 1934 based on a federal conviction for conspiracy to solicit contributions from federal and state employees. (Langer men had appeared on the NDAC campus, at the University, and the state mill and elevator soliciting "voluntary" subscriptions to the Non-Partisan League newspaper at five percent of one's salary.)

Steve Hagan, son of John Hagan, the Commissioner of Agriculture who also served on the State Board of Administration, was installed at NDAC in a newly created job, Secretary of the College. He coordinated the subscription drive and made voluntary appearances at the Legislature which undermined those of President Shepperd.

President Shepperd was continually badgered by the Board of Administration and members of the Legislature about the job NDAC was doing (this after a 59 percent cut in the College budget and a reduction in faculty salaries of over 50 percent). Shepperd resigned in 1937 with the intention of returning to his research in animal husbandry. John West, President of the University of North Dakota, was appointed Acting President of NDAC. The Board intended a consolidation of several departments at the two institutions. The same day letters of dismissal were sent to

seven NDAC employees, Robert Dolve, Dean of Engineering; Alba Bales, Dean of Home Economics; P.J. Olson, Assistant Dean of Agriculture; I.W. Smith, Professor of Mathematics and Dean of Men; Alfred Parrott, Registrar; N.D. Gorman, County Agent Leader for the Extension Service since 1924; and Jean Traynor, secretary to Presidents Shepperd, Coulter, and Ladd. Dr. H.L. Walster was relieved of his duties as Director of the Experiment Station and Extension Service and ordered to "confine his duties exclusively to the School of Agriculture." No charges were listed, no reasons given for the action. It was surmised that these people stood in Langer's way of controlling patronage with NDAC funds.

A year later, when the seven faculty members still had not had a hearing and no real charges had been made, the North Central Committee revoked the accreditation of

NDAC. It had taken until 1916 for the College to become accredited. Students were furious and joined in a successful statewide effort to initiate a measure to create a board of higher education insulated from political moves such as Langer's.

Frank Eversull, the President of Huron College, was named President of NDAC in 1938, and the College accreditation was eventually regained. The seven faculty members and Dean Walster were reinstated in their former positions. Some chose not to return.

Steve Hagan resigned as Secretary of the College shortly before it was disclosed that he had attempted to obtain an engineering degree by presenting bogus diplomas, some from non-existent institutions. John Hagan was defeated in the 1938 gubernatorial election. William Langer was elected to the U.S. Senate.

## The winter of '43: warm-hearted coeds and a North Dakota blizzard

For a time during the middle and late 1930s a compulsory ROTC was abolished at NDAC, and thoughts were far from war. By 1942 the campus was again the site for an officers candidate school and the Army Special Training Program (ASTP). A 1943 **Spectrum** article recalls the men of ASTP and the times they shared with the women of NDAC:

*"With 'I've got sixpence. . .' echoing through the air, a long line of young men from all parts of the USA started marching down Thirteenth Street. The skies were grey and wisps of snow whirled down from above. As we watched from our vantage point, a curious sense of emptiness came over us for*

*many of us had never seen real evidence of war before. Here we were watching boys march away whom we said we would be glad to see leave.*

*No longer would we have to stand the whistles and looks that greeted us as we entered the Science Hall. No longer would we blush under an 'eyes right' or be wakened by the early morning tramp of GI shoes. We can all sit down on a bus now and we don't have to sympathize with the boy who 'only got A minus' in a physics test.*

*But. . .still. . .an odd silence has fallen over the halls of NDAC. We shall miss taps at night and the songs they sang as they marched between classes. We were glad when it stormed so wholeheartedly some time ago because then we proved that we could have winter in North*

*Dakota, but secretly we were even more glad the sun was shining on Thursday. . . somehow it made the last day more pleasant to remember.*

*The friends we made are gone now. We did not realize how we would miss them when we wished them goodbye and good luck, but we were sincere in our wishes. Now as we walk down the quiet paths from class to class, with sudden sharp remembrance we hear the hymn of our state as it was sung by the boys marching away. . . Company A by the Field House . . .Company B advancing on perfect formation. . . remembering the candles at the Mess Hall. Perhaps it was their tribute to us. . .perhaps not. . . but we shall remember them as they were at that moment. . .a part of our state. . .our school . . .and our circle of friends."*

## Gold stars for "Doc"

He knew all about hot licks and jitterbugging. He went to the movies, performed rigorous calisthenics daily, and followed the Fargo-Moorhead Twins—when he was eighty. For thousands of students from 1904-1944, band leader Clarence "Doc" Putnam was "the greatest of them all."

His mother wanted him to be a doctor and Doc obliged her by attending Dartmouth and medical schools in Philadelphia and Chicago. Although he practiced medicine for twenty years, his overriding interest was music. For that his parents were perhaps equally responsible. When he was a baby, his mother laid him on a pillow behind the church organ when she sang in the choir. His father

led the band of the Eighth Regiment, Vermont Volunteers, and was killed in Sherman's march through Georgia during the Civil War. Doc took over the regiment band after the war and worked his way through college as a musician. (He also marched in seventy-three Memorial Day parades after his father's death.)

Doc practiced medicine in Moorhead, Ada, Superior, and Casselton before he came to Fargo. A fire destroyed his office in 1903 a few days after his insurance policy lapsed. Out of desperation he began teaching arithmetic, hygiene, and science classes at NDAC. He also taught music and gave lessons on the side before going full time with the music program. Although some attention had been paid to music as an extracurricular activity, the music department really grew up around Doc.

In 1915 when Putnam's military band turned out for its first inspection, there were fifteen in the ranks. After a decade, Doc was directing century bands, and the numerous superior ratings earned in ROTC inspections led to the name Gold Star Band.

Doc scouted the territory and worked hard to recruit good musicians. He found work for hundreds of them once they got to Fargo. "The man with the horn" leading the band attracted many including his successor, Bill Euren, and Harold Bachman, later well known as a composer and director of the Million Dollar Band.

Doc was 80 and still at work when he died in 1944. He wrote music that is remembered, "The Yellow and the Green" and the "North Dakota Hymn," but most of all Doc Putnam is loved and remembered by the AC/SU community as one of a kind, the greatest.

Doc and the Gold Star Concert Band in the newly built Field House, 1932.

Besides being a "band man,"
Doc maintained a College
symphony and a choral program
for both men and women.

NDAC students were often entertained by the live music of Doc and the band. This was a May Festival in the 1920s.

Doc sat next to his pupil and successor, Bill Euren, in this 1933 photo.

## Luke Bolley and the work at Plot 30

Fresh from Purdue with a tremendous desire to go to work, Henry Luke Bolley got off the train in Fargo in 1890, about a month after C.B. Waldron's arrival. A member of the original faculty, he remained at NDAC until his retirement in 1946. Bolley wrote the first Experiment Station bulletins, in which he described potato diseases and remedies, and he also began what was termed as classical studies of plant disease, especially with regard to flax.

Flax in the United States thrived only on new land, second crops yielding far less and the third crop failing completely. North Dakota was the last frontier for flax, and production nationwide seemed doomed. Bolley studied the current flax-sick land theories and came to the conclusion that soil fertility was not the problem but a fungus which he discovered, isolated and, named.

The U.S. Department of Agriculture Yearbook of 1936 claimed that Bolley had become perhaps the first man to subject agricultural crops to disease with the intent of breeding a hardier strain. The work was done on an eighth of an acre at the edge of campus called Plot 30. After the ground was infested with diseases hostile to flax, flax was planted there every year from the late 1890s. From a few bushels of selected seed came millions which in turn were planted across the nation. The USDA estimated in the 1930s that Bolley's flax seed had a value of $37,000,000.

Bolley made trips to Belgium, Germany, and Russia in 1903 to obtain seed to breed with strains at NDAC. In 1930 and 1931 he spent a year in Argentina selecting crop varieties for United States plant breeders. Bolley was sixty-six. Mrs. Bolley died on that trip to Argentina.

Luke Bolley also perfected several wheat varieties and discovered the cause of black stem rust, a parasite on the barberry bush. Due to his research and urging, the United States adopted national legislation and a plan for barberry eradication, North Dakota being the first state to adopt the program.

When he was not working at Plot 30, the former quarterback from Purdue coached and later managed the AC football team. The only Homecoming games he ever missed were in 1903, 1930 and 1931 when he traveled to Russia and South America.

Widely recognized as a scientist, Bolley was elected as a life member to the prestigious American Association for the Advancement of Science and received honorary doctor of science degrees from Purdue in 1937 and NDAC in 1938.

At Plot 30

Luke Bolley inspired generations of plant scientists from the time he was a young man traveling in Russia to his retirement nearly a half century later.

For many years the top student-athlete at NDAC was awarded the Bolley Medal. Bolley posed with his Purdue team in 1889.

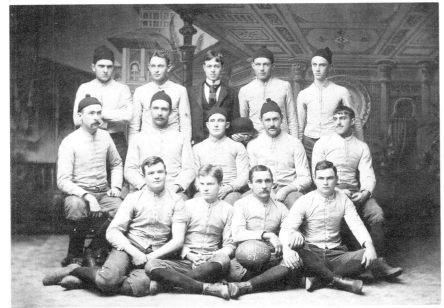

With Purdue team, second from left, front row

In Russia, 1903

### Life in Silver City

J.H. Longwell headed a committee in 1944 to make post-war plans. Among the committee's concerns were accommodations for regular students and education for veterans. Longwell had the opportunity to implement the plans when he became NDAC's seventh President in 1946.

Despite a postponement of fall registration due to a local poliomyelitis epidemic, over 2,300 persons entered the College in 1946. Student life returned to normal with crowded classrooms and overflowing dorms. The placing on campus of nearly one hundred trailers and sixty-five quonset-style houses slightly eased married-student housing.

Married students lived in quonsets and trailers about campus, and married faculty gathered in "temporary" housing across from Ceres Hall. Silver City gradually disappeared by the early 1970s. The faculty housing was destroyed in the tornado of 1957.

# A University on the Move

Someone once explained the popularity of the rocking chair—modern people are happiest when they are on the move; the rocking chair allows one to move even while sitting still.

The image one receives in reviewing the past thirty-five years at NDSU is motion. The University grew in many ways including the size of the student body, the number of faculty, and an enlarged physical plant. Sometimes the movement was with ideas, such as new programs. Occasionally the University merely rocked back and forth in a holding pattern, waiting for the Legislature to appropriate funds or additional students to make a critical mass for the next movement. On a few occasions the emphasis appears to have been placed on the back rather than the forth.

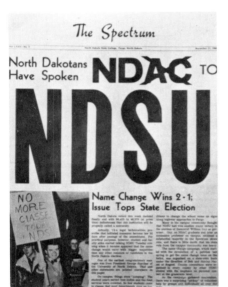

"What I saw made me sick. The place was run down. There wasn't a bit of paving." Although these words reflect Fred S. Hultz's first impression of the institution, he nevertheless accepted nomination and became President August 24, 1948. He saw his greatest challenge as the revitalization of the institution. To do this he needed to promote the school and generate publicity as well as persuade the Legislature to enlarge its appropriations for personnel and buildings. Hultz succeeded in accomplishing the tasks.

The student population also increased. In 1949 the student enrollment totaled 2,397, many of them veterans. The number declined immediately during the Korean conflict to a low of 1,679 in 1951 but rebounded until it had more than doubled in a decade, 3,581 in 1961. NDAC produced two Rhodes Scholars, Mancur Olson in 1954 and Gordon Kepner in 1958. In 1960 a team won the Intercollegiate Livestock Judging Contest at the International Live Stock and Grain Exposition in Chicago. In Festival Hall students listened to Victor Borge, Burl Ives, Duke Ellington, Dave Brubeck, Hal Holbrook, and Carlos Montoya; danced to the music of Wayne King, Jimmy Dorsey, and "Doc" Evans; or just enjoyed the sounds of Mantovani and his orchestra, Fred Waring, or the Boston Pops under the direction of Arthur Fiedler. The intercollegiate athletic teams, however, failed to move and often finished near the cellar.

More students necessitated more faculty. The old "greats" were retiring: T.E. Stoa, R.M. Dolve, Minnie Anderson, Lucile Horton, H.L. Walster, O.O. Churchill, Pearl Dinan, A.E. Minard, and O.A. Stevens, many of whom are recognized today by the buildings named for them. The new replaced the old and Hultz succeeded in raising the salaries by over 100 percent in the decade. New programs and new degrees became available: in 1959 the Doctor of Philosophy degree was authorized in plant science, animal science, pharmacy, entomology, and chemistry.

Not all faculty approved Hultz's leadership or style. Some believed he sacrificed salaries in order to enlarge the physical plant. The State Board of Higher Education research found that "there are a number who believe that the President is dictatorial and does not consult or advise with the faculty."

The Board, however, supported the President and agreed to request the resignation of four faculty members whom the President charged with "undermining" his way of running the institution. Cecil B. Haver, assistant professor of agricultural economics; Baldur Kristjanson, associate professor of agricultural economics; Daniel Posin, chair and professor of physics; and William Treumann, professor of chemistry. The firing was supported at a campus-held hearing but condemned by the AAUP which placed the institution on the censure list.

The college became a university under Hultz's administration. While the impetus for the change might have come from athletes who grew tired of being called "Moo U," others as early as the 1900s had advocated the new status that would symbolize that the institution was more than an "ag" college. The change did not come easily: when a constitutional amendment was defeated in 1958, the failure stimulated students and faculty to greater efforts. The second time the voters agreed and NDSU "was no longer bound to keep its non-technical complements under wraps."

Herbert Albrecht is reported to have said about a football team that had just finished a season 0-10, "we should be doing better." Albrecht, the new President, succeeded Fred Hultz who had died in April 1961.

As with football, other drastic changes occurred during Albrecht's tenure from 1961 to 1968. The institution witnessed a huge enrollment increase, from 3,581 in 1961 to 6,228 in 1968, an average yearly increase of 378 students.

Construction erupted on campus to accommodate the new students. The following is a partial listing of the new buildings:
1961: Burgum Hall, $530,000
1963: Reed-Johnson Hall, $1,344,000
       Weible Hall, $1,148,000
       Food Center, $700,000
1964: Memorial Union Addition, $600,000
       Dunbar Laboratories, $1,250,000
1965: Engineering and Architecture, $1,400,000
1966: Cereal Technology, $400,000
1967: Two High-Rise Dorms, $2,000,000
       Askanase Hall, $480,000

Changes occurred in the faculty as many new faces appeared. With the abolition of the old Council and the creation of the Faculty Senate, the governance of the faculty was altered. Albrecht said that "Democracy as practiced by a faculty senate many times drives administrators up the wall, but I know of no better way to secure a true academic environment than through substantial involvement of the faculty in university affairs." AAUP approved the new administration's governance structure and methods and removed NDSU from its list of censured institutions.

New academic programs were born and accredited. In 1966 the North Central Association extended full accreditation to the doctoral programs in entomology, animal science, plant science, chemistry, and pharmacy. NCA also renewed accreditation in all other areas. First steps were taken towards the Tri-College University and a Common Market approach to education.

Just doing better in football, however, is not what Albrecht had in mind. He wanted a winning team. He found a new coach, Darrell Mudra, and in two years the team went to 10-0.

In late 1967 Albrecht announced his decision to accept a position with the Ford Foundation and he became Director of the International Institute of Tropical Agriculture in Ibadan, Nigeria.

His tenure, brief though it was, provided the impetus and the foundation for the "Coming of Age" in the '70s and '80s.

The institution looked within to find its next leader, Laurel D. Loftsgard, an alumnus and the first native North Dakotan to be President of NDSU. Loftsgard, the tenth President, looked to the past in suggesting the future at his inauguration April 11, 1969:

I have the impression that during its early years, NDSU. . .was rather a brash young, no-nonsense kind of institution.

With its shirt sleeves rolled up, it was determined to do everything it could to help the North Dakota of that day survive.

In the intervening years, the University has followed most of the suggested directions. It has remained a "no-nonsense" institution that moves forward "with its shirt sleeves rolled up."

The moves, however, can hardly be described as "brash." The President often discusses the need for the "critical mass." It is summarized in the **Coming of Age** as "the situation which exists at a university. . .or department, when it had enough people, enough physical resources—buildings, equipment and other materials—and enough money to sustain the necessary chain reaction that will result in a superior educational experience."

Under Loftsgard, the institution continued to grow in all areas. In 1968 approximately 6,200 students attended NDSU; sixteen years later the numbers had grown to approximately 9,500. Construction on the physical plant continued:

1968: New Field House,
      $3,100,000
      Waldron Hall, $586,702
      Stevens Hall, $1,700,000
      Married-Student Housing,
      $3,206,000
1969: Sudro Hall Addition,
      $288,730
      Central Food Processing,
      $275,000
1971: Thorson Addition,
      $204,910
      West Dining Center,
      $957,640
1972: Third High Rise,
      $1,150,000
1973: Diagnostic Laboratory,
      $1,789,000
      Family Life Center/4-H,
      $2,250,000
1976: Askanase Hall Addition,
      $284,780
      Hultz Hall,
      $3,200,000
1977: Library Addition,
      $2,500,000
1979: Music Education Center,
      $5,000,000
1983: Northern Crops Institute,
      $1,400,000

Less noticeable than physical expansion and growth in enrollment, but equally important, has been the increased emphasis on the scholarship of students and faculty. After the successful 1975 completion of Project SU 75, a mostly "bricks and mortar" campaign, the next drive, called Century II, aims to establish an endowment which contributes to student scholarships and faculty development, especially critical as government funding for higher education is declining.

By 1980 over 40 merit scholars attended NDSU as a result of an effort to attract high calibre students. Substantial funds for faculty development and to improve classroom teaching have been awarded to NDSU by the Bush and Norwest Foundations.

The scientific and technical nature of NDSU took on greater importance in 1974 when the College of Science and Mathematics was formed and again in 1980 when the College of Engineering and Architecture became the University's largest with an enrollment exceeding 2,000. In agriculture the creation of the Northern Crops Institute has brought international trade teams to the campus and even more specialized research. Graduate education is up dramatically from the past.

How this critical mass of facilities and talent will fare in the future is not clear. That image is latent and remains to be seen.

# A Timeline: The Recent Years

## 1949

**February 6-12** Little Country Theatre celebrates thirty-five years. Highlighting the anniversary will be the presentation of "Around the Dawn," written by Mason Arvold, son of Director A.G. Arvold.

**March** Bison basketball, led by Dave Torson and Jack Garret, had an 11-13 record but tied for the cellar in NCI.

**Winter Qtr.** Grade point average for the term is 1.39, Freshman had 1.01, Seniors 1.78, Phi Kappa Phi 2.50, Sigma Phi Delta 1.34. Twenty-one persons had a 3.00 average.

**June 27- July 10** Paint Chemistry department, under Dr. Wouter Bosch, offers a short course in paint and varnishes. Twenty-three chemists from twelve states and Canada attended.

**Fall** Faculty adopt new academic regulations: 1) "F" now carries minus 1 honor points; 2) probation is determined by honor point average; freshmen are on probation if they earn less than .50; 3) suspension occurs if a student has two successive probations.

## 1950

**February 4** NDAC women's basketball team defeats Concordia, Moorhead State. Joy Aaser is leading scorer.

**Fall** Library is completed and ready for occupancy, Field House auditorium remodeled, Putnam Hall transformed from a library to a music hall, and Dacotah Field is moved.

**Fall** Fall enrollment totals 1,833, with about a three-to-one man-woman ratio, 301 decrease. Enrollment in 1920 was 375; 1930, 1,768; 1940, 1,973.

**November 9** Roy Rogers, Dale Evans, Trigger, and Bullet appear in the Field House. Proceeds go for the Student Union.

## 1951

**January 19** Jimmy Dorsey and his orchestra play for annual Military Ball.

**February 3** Saddle and Sirloin presents the 25th Little International Livestock Show. In addition to judging contests, the show features farm equipment demonstrations and coed cow-milking and hog-herding contests.

**Fall** Fall term enrollments for the state are: NDSU - 1,679; UND - 1,559; Minot State - 594; Valley City - 381; Wahpeton - 336; Dickinson State - 229; Mayville - 175; Ellendale - 91; Bottineau - 71.

**October 3** Drama Quartet, composed of Charles Laughton, Charles Boyer, Agnes Moorehead, Cedric Hardwicke, appears in Festival Hall.

**December** Campus groups donate blood plasma to help lower Korean casualty list.

## 1952

**February 29** Bison basketball team wins NCC title. Coaches name Art Bunker and Don Fougner to All-Conference team.

**May 20** Duke Ellington presents a concert in Festival Hall.

**September 17** Bids let for new $400,000 women's dormitory to be located behind Festival.

**Fall** Fall enrollment reaches 1,731 including 352 women. Engineering and Agriculture have one woman each, Chemistry 6, Arts and Sciences 90, Pharmacy 11, and Home Economics 242 (and no men).

## 1953

**February 27** First ugliest man on campus contest held; Clyde Chappel wins.

**Spring Qtr.** Campus radio station begins broadcasting from 5 p.m. to 7 p.m. every weekday.

**June-July** Seven short courses offered including two paint courses. Paint courses filled with persons from thirteen states, three countries. Dr. Daniel Posin teaches an evening course in radio and television.

**Fall** New buildings nearing completion are the Home Economics building and the Student Union. Charles Laughton directs "John Brown's Body" at the Field House. The cast includes Tyrone Power, Anne Baxter, and Raymond Massey.

**October 29- October 30** Joyce Swenson elected Queen of annual Homecoming. Twenty-one floats, twenty-three cars, and five bands are in the parade, but UND cops the Nickel Trophy 26-6. Football team finishes with a 2-4 NCC record. Student Union has its grand opening.

**November 25** "The Robe," the first cinemascope film, opens at the Fargo Theatre and stars Richard Burton, Jean Simmons, and Victor Mature.

## 1954

**February 4** ATO Beauties edge Gamma Phi Beasts 21-20 in the annual Bromo Bowl; $70.25 ticket sales donated to March of Dimes.

**May** State Board drops geology and geography from curriculum. Students, administrators, and townspeople petition the Board for their reinstatement.

**Fall** Frank Mirgain replaces R.M. Dolve as Dean of Engineering and Caroline Budewig is named new Home Economics Dean.

## 1955

**February 26** ATO Beauties beat the Beasts of Gamma Phi 13-6 in annual Bromo Bowl playing in 24-below weather and four feet of snow.

**March 4** NDAC basketball team finishes in second place in the NCC. Duane Anderson wins the Rahjah Trophy and places sixth in the conference in scoring.

**Fall** Fall enrollment reaches 2,401 including about 600 veterans from the Korean GI Bill. Weekly campus cuties include Joan Nelson, Janet Monson, Judy Hunstad, Phyllis Diede, Maureen Stegman, Sandra Benedict, Karen Eddiger, and Genevieve Kovell. KDSC is found at 790 on the dial. Deejays include Chuck Phillips, Arlene Olson, and Ward Dunkirk.

## 1956

**March 3** John Johnson and Reggie Gorder will manage the 30th Little International. Joan Stammen is chosen Queen. Special entertainment includes the "Kow Kollege Five Plus Two Minus Three."

**Fall** Students are offered the opportunity to receive three polio vaccination shots at $1.25 each.

**December 7** Greyhound rates advertised in **Spectrum** include round-trip fares to Valley City $2.90, Bismarck $8.55, Twin Cities $8.65, New York City $57.80. The College Inn, Monday Nite Special, Turkey With Trimmings, is $.85.

## 1957

**Spring** Farmers Union Co-op House, under construction at 12th Street and 12th Avenue North, will house forty-four students.

**June 20** Tornado hits campus, College Y is a shambles.

**Fall** Burt Brandrud, Director of Admissions, announces that enrollment tops 3,000: 2,511 men and 552 women. Lettermen enforce beanie tradition, freshmen not wearing the proper headwear are imprisoned until they sing the Green and Yellow.

**October** Debate team meets team from Cambridge with question "This house deplores the modern preoccupation with material progress." John Pancratz and Don Schreder represent NDAC. Flu hits campus, 300-400 students absent every day last week of the month. Football game

between Augustana and NDAC is cancelled.

## 1958

**Winter Qtr.** Varsity college wrestling comes to NDAC; compiled a 2-8 dual record. Tom Neuberger is coach.

**April 19** Board of Higher Education rejects name change proposal on the grounds that it will take a constitutional amendment to change the name.

**November 4** North Dakota voters reject a measure that would have changed the name of the institution to State University. Voters also defeated a one-mill levy measure; revenue would have been used to pay for new buildings at state schools.

## 1959

**May 8-9** Sharivar, with Bison Brevities, plays, debates, open houses, and shows, was attended by more than 2,000 guests.

**Summer** Work starts on a new $660,000 Pharmacy building and a $750,000 Agricultural Science building. In addition several other buildings, including an addition to the Union, a men's dormitory, a women's dormitory, and married-student housing are scheduled for construction using non-appropriated funds. Almost 100 courses plus six special courses are scheduled for Summer School June 8 to July 18.

**Fall** Dr. John Hove is named head of the Department of English. Other appointments

include: Dr. John Brophy, Geology; Marillyn Nass, Physical Education; and Don Schwartz, Communication. TV course is offered to students. Dr. Gerry Walz, Professor of Education and Psychology, is the instructor of the first locally produced college-level TV course.

**October 16-17** Carol Olson is Homecoming Queen. Festivities began October 14 with a bonfire and snake dance. Ross Fortier and Curt Quenette are football co-captains. Bisons lose to UND 15-20. But the team will post its best record in thirteen years by finishing with a 3-1-2 record and second place in the NCC.

**October 23** State group is formed to back name change.

## 1960

**March 18** Marv Bachmeier breaks four league basketball records including total points (338), average (28.2), field goals (119), and one game (47). He also is named to the Little All-American Team by the Associated Press.

**Spring** Bowling team has 20-6 record, with an individual average of 181. The team finished twelfth in a national tournament.

**June 13-** Summer **August 15** Institute for seventy high school science and mathematics teachers is held. The Institute is made possible by a $93,700 grant from the National Science Institute. Dr. F.L. Minnear is director.

**November** North Dakota voters approve initiated measure to

change name of NDAC to NDSU by two to one margin. Bill Guy, '41, is elected governor, Robert and Shirley Nasset led the alumni, and Robert Crom, Director of Communications, directed the drive for a name change.

## 1961

**February 3** Survey indicates that there are 634 stuffed animals in the women's dorms; Ceres Hall leads all with 369.

**April 28** Reed Hall, originally to be placed south of Minard, is relocated north of Sudro. Burgum is to be built east of Putnam as planned. Students had protested both locations.

**May 5** Paul Kozieg holds campus limbo record at twenty-five inches.

**Spring** Bowling team compiles 24-4 record and sets a national collegiate scoring record, rolling a total of 3,177 in a match with Mankato State.

**October 2** NDSU enters the computer age when it installs an IBM 1620.

**October 21** William Hunter's **Beacon Across the Prairie,** a history of the institution, is released, coinciding with Homecoming and the Land-Grant Centennial. Dorothy Vorwerk is named Queen but the Bison will not earn the Nickel Trophy.

**November 18** Bob Lervick and Jackie Boelter win Gus XXIV, traditionally given to some lucky couple at the Spinster Skip.

## 1962

**April 6** Blue Key sponsors **Damn Yankees,** directed by Bryan Gackle and featuring Bruce Anderson as Joe Hardy. Marillyn Nass, assistant professor of Physical Education, is the choreographer.

**April 28** Sharivar's featured speaker is Governor Bill Guy. Among the activities are go-cart races near Shepperd Arena, bowling tournament, and displays and demonstrations by all colleges. Some students, however, question the value of the program intended for high school seniors.

## 1963

**January** Basketball team reaches century mark for the first time, 104-68, against Morningside. Ron McLeod tallied 24 and Wayne Langen 20. The team, however, will finish in the cellar.

**February 15-16** Sue Haas reigns over the 37th Little International. Activities include the Hall of Fame Banquet, Engineering and Home Economics show, showmanship contest, and co-ed greased-pig contest. Ray Meyer is manager and Gary Knutson was selected grand champion showman.

**February 27** The first oral polio vaccine clinic is held on campus; President Albrecht proclaimed it "Sugar Lump Wednesday."

**March 27** State Board of Higher Education increases tuition from $120 per quarter to $180.

**April 3** Destruction of Dakota Hall begins; constructed in 1919, the "temporary" building was originally intended to house soldiers.

## 1964

**May 13** Raids on women's dorms net an estimated $1,000 worth of undergarments.

**September 16** Dacotah Inn opens in the Memorial Union. Luncheon and dinner require tie and dress clothes.

**October 8-10** Homecoming features performances by Ray Charles and the Four Lads. The Rahjahs began three snake dances to converge on the field where Queen Lane Gunner was crowned. Frank Hentges, quarterback, and Mike Cichy were selected as players of the week in a 42-7 victory over Augustana.

## 1965

**January 20** Dunbar Laboratories are finally completed; strike during 1964 delayed the work.

**February 17** Bob Blasey, freshman, is the only male among 437 co-eds in the College of Home Economics.

**March 31** Rifle Team wins first place at the Intercollegiate Sectional Pistol and Rifle matches; James Dramstand led the team.

## 1966

**September 14** Laurel Loftsgard is appointed Vice-President for Academic Affairs.

**October 2** The University of Oklahoma defeats NDSU college bowl team 375-345. David Knutson is captain, Catherine Cater is coach.

**November 4** Simon and Garfunkel concert is held at the Field House.

**November 5** Bison's twenty-four game unbeaten football streak is ended by San Diego State 36-0.

**November 23** "Common Market" classes begin with five NDSU students taking classes at MSU and two MSU students at NDSU.

## 1967

**March 15** "Special Interest Day" brings to campus Ralph Abernathy and George Lincoln Rockwell.

**May 10** Viet Nam teach-in panel includes Carmen Lodise, Economics; John Bond, Political Science; and John Hove, English.

**October 12** The Rahjah Club is placed on probation by the Student Senate for conduct of its members. The **Spectrum** headlines read "Rahjah: Asset or Perennial Embarrassment?"

**October 18** The Mitchell Trio with John Denver appears in concert as part of Homecoming activities.

## 1968

**March 8-10** "Treasure Island" is the last play in the Old Main Little Country Theatre. Since 1914 LCT has had approximately 400 plays and 1,600 performances.

**April** Fargo-Moorhead draws presidential hopefuls including Robert Kennedy, Richard Nixon, Eugene McCarthy, and Hubert Humphrey.

**April 1** Ceres Hall residents found a Volkswagen parked in the first floor hallway.

**September 26** Rahjahs obtain the hearse owned by the Golden Feathers of UND.

**October 21** David Worden, chair of physics, is appointed Vice President for Academic Affairs.

**December 14** The Bison, under Coach Ron Erhardt, win the Pecan Bowl by defeating Arkansas State 23-14.

**Fall-Winter** Protest increases over the nation's involvement in Viet Nam. **Notes from the Underground,** a protest newspaper, appears.

## 1969

**April 17** "The students have saved Fargo so far," reports a Fargo official as the Red River crested at 37.3 feet, the highest since 1897.

**September** City Commission denies parade permit to Viet Nam Action Committee (VAC) for an antiwar demonstration. VAC will lead an antiwar protest and demonstration again when Vice President Spiro Agnew visits Fargo.

**November** The Bison football team wins its sixth consecutive NCC title, third consecutive bowl bid, and second consecutive national championship.

## 1970

**January 15** C.M. Swallers is conducting research on production "of a relatively new crop," the sunflower.

**February 26** Student Senate votes overwhelmingly for a resolution calling for the replacement of the current toilet tissues with a "soft, squeezable" brand.

**September 18** Bill Russel captivates audience as the highlight speaker of the fall orientation program. Co-ed living is initiated in Sevrinson Hall.

**October 7-10** The Little Country Theatre presents "The Man of LaMancha," starring Gary Schneider and Dan McDermott. It is directed by Fred Walsh and costumed by Don Larew. The Bison football team extends its winning streak to twenty-five games defeating Augustana 45-7 before a Homecoming crowd of 8,000. Chris Hogan is named Queen.

## 1971

**March 16** Led by Bill DeMaray and Bob Backlund, NDSU places fourth in NCAA College Division National Wrestling Tournament. Bucky Maughan is voted runner-up Coach of the Year.

**April 30-May 2** The 11th Annual Blue Key musical features "Brigadoon" starring Steven Stark and Donna Wassmund.

**October 1** Tin City quonset huts are placed on sale for $150 each.

**November 5** Coal strike forces heat cutbacks. The University has coal supplies for about fifteen days.

**November 16** Mike Slack wins first place at NCAA College Division cross country; NDSU's team finishes second. Slack will finish third at the university division level.

## 1972

**March 14** The Robert Odney Award, to be given for good teaching, is established. Pat Beatty receives the first honor.

**April 13** Neil Jacobsen, Director of Student Academic Affairs in the College of Arts and Sciences, is appointed Dean of the newly formed College of University Studies.

**June 4** The Prairie Stage Company takes to the road under the direction of Fred Walsh; shows include "The Fantasticks," "Pinnochio," and "The Peripatetic Bartholomew Bone."

**September 26** The Resident Heads charge fees to open dorm doors at Weible and Burgum Halls, 10¢ and 15¢ each time.

**December 5** Phil Rognlie announces plan to start an Upward Bound program for veterans.

## 1973

**January 31** Tie for an off-campus Student Senate seat is broken by a fight-to-the-finish game of Monopoly; Jeff Gehrke forced Steve Bolme into bankruptcy after seventy-two minutes.

**March 9** An all-University informational session is held to explain the 1973-1975 budget and a plan for University reorganization including creating a new College of Science and Mathematics.

**March 25** The Erhardt era comes to an end when Ron Erhardt accepts a position with the New England Patriots. He leaves with six NCC championships in seven years, four post-season bowl games, two national championships, and a 67-7-1 record.

**October 20** Barbara Jo Thomas is Homecoming Queen; Grand Funk performs in concert; NDSU defeats UND before 13,500 fans; and five fraternities lose their toilets to Ron's Plumbing and Sanitation.

## 1974

**February 12** The First Annual Erotic Film Festival is shown on campus.

**March 21** Seventeen couples complete a forty-hour dance marathon to raise money for Multiple Sclerosis.

**May** The comedy team of Cheech and Chong presents a show at the Old Field House described by the **Spectrum** as "remarkable only for its bad taste."

**Fall** Bill Blain, former associate director of the UND student center, is chosen to become head of the Union.

## 1975

**April** Harriett Light awarded a Bush Fellowship to pursue a doctoral degree at Michigan State University.

**May** Tari Joyce, a Fargo co-ed and member of the swimming team, becomes the first woman to win a varsity letter in intercollegiate athletics.

**June** North Dakota-Minnesota reciprocity program becomes a reality; students from Minnesota attending NDSU no longer must pay out-of-state tuition.

**July 1** Joseph Stanislao, professor and Associate Dean at Cleveland State College, is named as Dean of the College of Engineering and Architecture.

**Fall** Cost for the twenty-meal food contracts increases to $215 per quarter. Enrollment reaches a new record with 6,957 students.

**November 29** Mike Bishop is named 1975 High Individual at Chicago International Livestock Judging contest with the team placing eighth overall.

## 1976

**June 7** The Prairie Stage embarks for the last time for ten North Dakota communities. With Fred Walsh as the major force behind it, the Stage played to more than 50,000 people in the 50'x 50' green and yellow tent.

**August** With the gift of an electronic carillon by Robert and Paula Verne Parrott, chimes are once again heard on campus after an absence of approximately a quarter of a century.

**Fall** The Graver Inn, with 110 rooms, is acquired to house men students, a move to help relieve an acute shortage of student housing. The Inn was acquired through a gift-purchase arrangement by the NDSU Development Foundation.

**September 24** Van Es Hall removed.

**October 8** Twelfth Avenue bridge over the railroad tracks is slated for demolition and replacement. Students, however, express concern about the possibility of increased traffic.

## 1977

**March 2** The National League of Nursing accredits the Associate Degree Nursing Program.

**April 27** The Fargo business community funds the "Chamber of Commerce Distinguished Professorship" program. The award is accompanied by $5,000. S. S. Maan becomes the first recipient.

**May 6** Bison Brevities returns after nearly two decades.

**Summer** Professors retiring this year include Corwin Roach, History and Religion and Director of the North Dakota School of Religion; W.J. Promersberger, chair of the Agricultural Engineering Department; and Constance West, Speech and Drama Department. Eleanor Evanson, administrative assistant and head secretary in the Student Affairs Office, retires after nearly thirty-nine years.

**Summer-Fall** Appointed to new positions are George Pratt, Chair, Agricultural Engineering Department; John McCune,

Provost, Tri-College University; John Helgeland, Director, North Dakota School of Religion; and Sandra Holbrook, Equal Opportunity Office.

## 1978

**January 8** NDSU enters the age of conservation and in one year saved enough coal to fill 93 train cars, electricity to serve 84 family dwellings for a year, and water to meet the needs of 232 families for a year.

**March 16** The Gold Star Band returns from a two-week tour with performances in Montana, Oregon, and Washington.

**Summer** Erv Inniger named head basketball coach, Donna Palivec volleyball coach.

**September 8** Record enrollment with more than 7,600 students causes more than 300 students to be assigned to temporary quarters.

**October** Les Hirchert, the Memorial Union's barber, begins his twenty-fifth year, the only person in the Union who has been here since it was built in 1953.

## 1979

**January** Don Morton named head football coach replacing Jim Wacker who has accepted head coaching position at Southwest Texas. Roald Lund named Dean of the College of Agriculture and Director of the Agricultural Experiment Station.

**January 31-February 3** The Little Country Theatre presents "The Amorous Flea." Directed by Tal Russell, Robert Littlefield plays the main character. Don

Larew designs the set for his sixty-eighth production.

**April 10** Glenn Smith, former Dean of the Graduate School and professor of agronomy, receives the Blue Key Doctor of Service Award. His work in breeding plants has resulted in releases of five durum-wheat varieties and four hard-red spring-wheat varieties.

**June 25-28** The 14th Rare Earth Research Conference, chaired by John Gruber, Dean of the College of Science and Mathematics, is held bringing together 250 scientists from twenty-two different countries.

**May 22** Degrees are awarded to 1,437 students: 25 doctoral, 104 associate's, 157 master's, and 1,151 bachelor's.

**Fall** Nick's Place and the General Store open to serve the campus community.

## 1980

**February 15-16** The 54th Little I held. Dr. V.K. "Doc" Johnson has been advisor to the Saddle and Sirloin Club for the past seventeen years. Julie Johnson is Queen, Dennis McCoy and David Fleming emerge as overall Grand Champions in the 32nd Agricultural Engineering Show.

**May 16** H.R. Hoops named Vice President for Academic Affairs.

**May 23** The 2.7 million addition to the Library is dedicated. The Library now contains 337,000 volumes and a staff of forty-two members.

**September 9** Three Fargo motels, Motel 75, Econ-O-Tel, and Thrifty Scot, are housing approximately one hundred male students.

**October 9** Fund Fair held in conjunction with Homecoming. Events include a tuck-in service, face painting, dunking booth, cow-chip throwing booth, and pie throwing. Funds are donated to the local Rape and Abuse Crisis Center.

**November 18** First women's swimming team fielded, losing to UND 59-56 in a dual meet. Members include Geri Eng, Leola Daul, Amy Krieg, and Kathy Tyvand. Another issue of Wrecked'Em is published.

## 1981

**April 14** Speech team places ninth among 102 schools at the National Pi Kappa Delta convention. LaVonne Lussenden places first in informative speaking, second in discussion, and third in oratory.

**May 15** Mary Bromel, professor of bacteriology, is 47th recipient of the Blue Key Doctor of Service Award; Zeno Wicks, Chair, Polymers and Coatings Department, awarded 1981 Fargo Chamber of Commerce Distinguished Professor; and Robert Koob is named Dean of the College of Science and Mathematics.

**Summer** North Dakota Repertory Theatre begins performance; Tal Russell is the director.

**Fall** Those named to new positions include: Roger Kerns,

Director of Student Academic Affairs; Gwendoline Brown, Chair, Department of Food and Nutrition; Denis Isrow, Associate Director of the Division of HPER/A; Joseph Norwood, Dean of Pharmacy; Charlotte Bennett, Assistant Dean, College of Home Economics.

**December 12** NCAA Division II Championship goes to former Coach Jim Wacker and Southwest Texas State when they defeated Don Morton and NDSU 42-13 at the Palm Bowl.

## 1982

**March** Bucky Maughan's eight-man team captures second at Division II National Tournament with Mike Langlais placing first in his weight. Women's basketball team loses to Charleston College in the semifinals.

**April 1** Weible women raid Reed-Johnson on "panty-raid"; end of month men lead raid on Thompson.

**April 2** Air Force ROTC celebrates thirty-fifth year at NDSU.

**April 22-24** Blue Key sponsors fiftieth edition of the Bison Brevities. The Newman Center wins the Best Production Award. More than 125 individuals participated in twelve acts. The 1982 edition is the last in Festival Hall.

**May** The new Music Building opens. Nine faculty, serving a total of 237 years, retire, including John Brophy, Geology; Catherine Cater, English; Beulah Gregoire, HPER/A; Richard Lyons,

English; Frank Cassel, Zoology; Richard Witz, Agricultural Engineering; Arnold Schooler, Agronomy; and Hollis Omodt, Soils.

**October 14-17** Homecoming 1982 features dedication of the Reineke Fine Arts Center, the Gold Star Marching Band, Kelvin Wynn and Lisa Diemert as royalty, and a 21-14 victory over UND before 11,600 fans at Dacotah Field.

## 1983

**January 11** Ithel Schipper, Professor of Veterinary Science receives the twenty-seventh annual Faculty Lectureship Award.

**February 27-28** The NCAA Division I Wrestling Championships are held on campus with Bucky Maughan's team placing second.

**Fall 1983** Main Campus enrollment reaches 9,477 compared with 7,619 for 1979.

**December 10** Bison football team defeats the Central State Marauders of Wilberforce, Ohio in the Palm Bowl to win the NCAA Division II championship.

## 1984

**February 10-11** The fifty-eighth Little International takes place with such events as livestock showmanship and ham curing contests as well as the thirty-sixth Agricultural Engineering show.

**April 9** H. Ray Hoops, Vice President for Academic Affairs, named president of South Dakota State University.

**April 27-29** The fifty-second production of Bison Brevities is held in Festival Concert Hall. This year's show consists of three fifteen-minute production acts and nine curtain acts.

**May 26** Ninetieth annual commencement exercises are held with 1,326 receiving bachelor degrees, 256 master degrees, 133 associate degrees and 22 doctoral degrees.

**June 9** State Board of Higher Education approves the use of $476,000 from a tuition surcharge for the purchase of 171 microcomputers to be installed in clusters across the campus for student use.

**October 12** Plans for the Robert Perkins Engineering Center for Technology Transfer are announced. The center is a cooperative venture by NDSU, the North Dakota Economic Development Commission and the Control Data Corporation (CDC) of Minneapolis with access to CDC information networks and data bases worldwide.

**December 8** A 50-yard fieldgoal on the last play of the game lifts Troy State of Alabama over the Bison National Division II football title at the Palm Bowl in McAllen, Texas.

**December 31** Robert Koob, Dean of Science and Mathematics, is named Academic Vice President.

# The Recent Years

## 1949 -1984

## Farewell, "Old Green and Yellow"

Archibald Minard served the College for forty-six years. A Harvard graduate, Minard was hired in 1904 to teach freshman English, which he did to all twenty-five students. Three years later he became head of the English Department. In 1919 he was appointed Dean of the School of Science and Literature, a position he held until his retirement in 1950.

Dean Minard was affectionately known to NDAC students as "Old Green and Yellow," for his part in writing the words to the college hymn. His lifetime of service to NDAC was recognized when Science Hall was renamed in his honor.

## A tribute to Doc

With the completion of the Library, the Music Building, once called a brick doghouse by **Forum** writer Jim Baccus, was torn down and the department moved to renovated Putnam Hall, named for Doc Putnam. Mrs. Putnam and members of the family were on hand for the rededication.

Choir Director and head of the Music Department, Ernst van Vlissingen, and his staff look pleased to be in their new home. Bill Euren, who succeeded Doc Putnam, is seated on Van's left.

The first stage of the union was completed in 1953, and an addition was built a decade later.

The Bison Grill became a regular stop on the campus itinerary.

## Home Economics builds, grows

Shortly after the completion of the Student Union, the nearby Home Economics building was opened in 1954. The $400,000 building was called a "dream come true" at its dedication. In the next decade enrollment in home economics went from a few hundred to more than 1,000, space once again becoming a problem.

Elvira Smith, the first to head the Food and Nutrition Department, began at NDAC in 1923 and served until 1960 when Mavis Nymon succeeded her.

Lucile Horton, the first to head the Home Economics Education Department, remained at the college from 1929-1960.

Emily Reynolds succeeded Minnie Anderson as head of Textiles and Clothing and served in that position until her retirement in 1980.

During the 1950s home economics students kept the spirit of college extension with Saturday morning broadcasts over KFGO.

Reynolds

Horton

Smith

## Chemistry and Physics

Alfred Rheineck directed the coatings science program, a legacy of Ladd's paint studies and well known in its own right in the field.

Joel Broberg was a favorite among NDSU students for his teaching of the large introductory chemistry sections.

Daniel Posin, a physicist, did not stay long as he and three others were fired by President Hultz. The removals were judged legal but cause for censure by the American Association of University Professors.

For many years Dr. Fred Sands delighted his introductory chemistry classes with "Mr. Wizard" demonstrations.

Rheineck

Broberg

Posin

Sands

## Agriculture: Still noble and healthy

The outsider might sense an air of self-righteousness in the sayings on the corridor walls of Morrill Hall, but Washington's sentiments seem borne out in this photo of a proud father and son with their prize animal.

## L.R. Waldron:
## He was a Midas

L.R. Waldron's career in agriculture lasted well into the postwar era, beginning at NDAC in 1899 and ending in 1952.

"Out of the ruins of past disaster new values have been developed for the future" is how L.R. Waldron described his work on the development of a new strain of stem rust-resistant wheat. He is best known for the development of Ceres, Rival, and Mida strains of wheat that added millions to the nation's farm economy.

Dr. Waldron was a Fellow of the Linnean Society of London, but William Hunter also remembers Waldron as the possessor of "an encyclopaedic knowledge of many subjects outside his own field." Hunter and Waldron were teammates on a radio program called "Stump the Professors." "Dr. Waldron could answer many more questions than any one of the rest of the group."

In 1954 L.R. Waldron planned the wheat breeding program so ably continued by his successor, Dr. Glenn Smith.

Stoa

Walster

Hazen

Norum

Bolin

DeAlton

Lana

## H.L. Walster, leader

From 1919-1954 Harlow Walster greatly influenced NDAC. He broadened the curriculum in agriculture when he became Dean of Agriculture in 1924. He was also a chairman of agronomy, producing original research. In the '30s he took on the job of running both the Extension Service and the Experiment Station when funds were scarce and consolidation was forced upon the College.

An active public speaker, Walster lectured on a wide range of subjects including tax research, land use, science and agriculture, soils, waste and irrigation, and the history of agriculture.

In 1953 Dean Walster was awarded an honorary doctor of science degree and the new agriculture science building, the present home of agronomy, was named for him.

Arlon Hazen became Dean of Agriculture in 1957 after a short term by Glenn C. Holm.

Some of Hazen's veterans included Enoch Norum, soils; F.M. Bolin, veterinary science; and Ernest DeAlton, agricultural education. Edwin Lana arrived in 1956 to be head of horticulture. Ted Stoa retired as chairman of agronomy in 1960 after a career that began at NDAC in 1921.

The machinery has been scaled up since Bill Promersberger taught this agricultural engineering class.

An entomology class studied the *Apis mellifera* (honeybee). Chickens are no longer shown in the Little International as they were in 1957.

## An AC/SU family

In 1877 Frank Johnson was on his way back to Ohio from the gold fields of South Dakota when the train stopped in Casselton. He got off, walked a couple miles north of town and decided to homestead. The Johnson family has farmed there ever since.

Johnson's son, Roy Sr., was a member of the first State Board of Higher Education. From 1938-1954 he was the designated NDAC representative on the Board, and he represented the College well, fighting hard for its interests. A graduate of the University of Minnesota and former Speaker of the House in North Dakota, Mr. Johnson was awarded an honorary Doctor of Science degree at the 1956 NDAC Commencement.

Johnson's sons, Ralph '48, Roy '50, and many other members of the Johnson family have long been devoted to NDSU.

## Cigars and sodas give way to science

The pharmacists who journeyed into North Dakota in territorial days set up their cigar counters and soda fountains and compounded drugs with a modicum of education and licensing requirements. But the North Dakota Pharmaceutical Association organized by 1886 and in 1899 they asked Professor Ladd to address them on the topic of pharmacy education. By 1901 President Worst and Professor Ladd got the go-ahead to begin offering two-and four-year courses in pharmacy.

It was thought that the College was the appropriate place for the teaching of pharmacy since Ladd had established food and drug labs there. For several years pharmacy was a part of the School of Chemistry. In 1908 William F. Sudro, a graduate of the University of Michigan, came to NDAC to teach pharmacy. By 1919 pharmacy was made a separate school, and, with a few exceptions during brief periods of reorganization, Sudro served as its dean until 1955.

Sudro

During Sudro's forty-seven years at the College, pharmacy had a strong reputation and its enrollment steadily grew. Dean Sudro was awarded an honorary Doctor of Science degree at the 1955 commencement. When the School of Pharmacy was moved from Francis Hall to its new building in 1960, the facility was named in his honor.

Dean Clifton Miller led the new regime in Sudro Hall. The school was organized into several departments including pharmacology, pharmacy administration, pharmacognacy, and toxicology.

Muriel Vincent and Leo Schermeister, now veterans of the college, joined the faculty in 1958.

Vincent

Miller

Schermeister

**The summer of 1957**
On June 20, 1957, a tornado
swept across the Golden Ridge
section of northwest Fargo
damaging much of the city and
taking lives. The campus lay in
its path.

Silver City was flattened, parts of
Festival Hall were lost, and the
campus YMCA destroyed. The
roof from the nearby Hasty
Tasty disappeared and rubble
heaped in front of the College
entrance.

## Shake, rattle and roll!

The Beaux Arts Ball of 1951 anticipated space exploration of a decade later. By mid-decade the major source of pinups in men's dorms was **Playboy.** About the same time a more innocent pastime, the Hoola Hoop, was in vogue. By 1958 Elvis had arrived, and students were taken with something new called rock and roll.

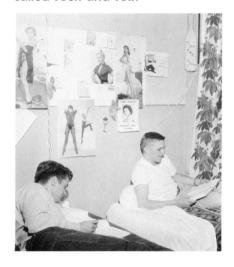

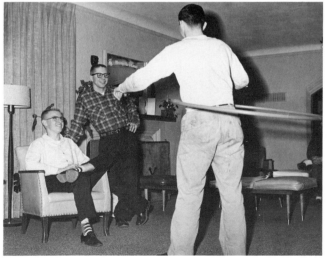

### Sharivar

Sharivar was a means of letting high school students "share in varsity life" at their new state university. Fraternities and sororities got an early jump on fall rush, and the colleges held open house. This gravity-defying demonstration was intended to attract prospective engineers.

## AC/SU

Some people today say they wish they had never changed the name of North Dakota Agricultural College. History professor Bill Reid is one of them. He says the name was distinctive, especially now that we are in an age of proliferating state universities.

Those who fought for the college name change, including agricultural interests, would hardly agree, but it is true that the mention of "AC" or "Moo U" does not raise the hackles as it once did. There is an appreciation at NDSU for the science of agriculture and what it means to the state, and the Aggies mix confidently with a diverse student population.

Efforts to change the name of NDAC began in the early part of the century, and the name North Dakota State College was informally adopted in the '20s. An initiated measure to change the name in 1958 failed, but the friends of the College campaigned hard the next time, and the measure passed in 1961. On the letterhead it is officially North Dakota State University of Agriculture and Applied Sciences. For others it's simply SU. For a few it will always be the AC, a name with an honorable history.

## Albrecht succeeds Hultz, 1961-1969

Dr. Herbert R. Albrecht became ninth President in October, succeeding Fred Hultz who died in April 1961. Although his tenure witnessed great academic advancements and growth in the physical plant as well as the student body, Albrecht is probably best remembered for changing the fortunes of the football program at NDSU.

Dean Frank Mirgain and President Albrecht broke ground in a more than symbolic way for the new engineering complex, completed in 1965.

## Engineering and Architecture enter a new age

With a computer, an adjacent wind tunnel, and labs where engineers could penetrate the mysteries of the trapezoidal wier, the College of Engineering was entering a new age. The tweedy professorial look of civil engineer John Oakey with his transit is a comforting reminder that some things change less radically.

Ernie Anderson

A.W. Anderson

Ed Anderson

Recently retired veterans in electrical engineering are Ernie Anderson and Ed Anderson, both arrivals in the late '40s. Knute Henning was long-time chairman of architecture as was A.W. Anderson for mechanical engineering. Harold Jenkinson continues to teach architecture. R.K. Wattson was a professor of aeronautical engineering.

Jenkinson

Henning

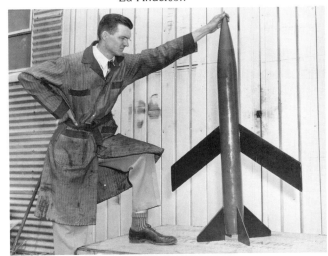

Wattson

## Dunbar Laboratories and the USDA build

Science education and research at NDSU took a great stride forward in 1964 with the completion of Dunbar Laboratories, a new chemistry complex. The building was named for Ralph Dunbar, Dean of Chemistry from 1943-1960. Dunbar, who joined the faculty in 1937, was the editor of a chemistry encyclopedia, the author or co-author of several textbooks, and a frequent contributor to national journals of chemistry.

The following year the USDA Radiation and Metabolism Laboratory was completed on the northwest corner of the campus. Several of its staff hold adjunct positions with the University.

Hertel

Schoff

Russell

Schwartz

Sackett

Pettee

## Arts and Sciences — from strictly service to professional

Seth Russell became Dean of Arts and Sciences in 1953. A sociologist, he was committed to the idea that the University can make a difference in its constituents' lives. He often traveled and spoke to audiences throughout the state.

Russell's most difficult job was upgrading the college of Arts and Sciences from a group of miscellaneous departments with only service courses to a higher professional level.

The faculty of the College of Arts and Sciences dated from E.W. Pettee of economics and Leonard Sackett in English. They began in 1928 and 1929. Sackett also collected information for the Institute for Regional Studies. (Masonry was a hobby.) Leo Hertel was chairman of modern languages and editor of the Institute's publications. Donald Schwartz was chairman of communication. Francis Schoff taught English and wrote reviews of cultural events for **The Forum.**

## Twist and shout!

In the '60s students would twist and shout and strain to get under the limbo stick. The formal military balls survived as did the zanier Beaux Arts balls.

## Winning football and national championships

The President "believed we could do better" in football and indeed the team did improve during the 1960s. Darrell Mudra, hired from Colorado, filled the stands with spectators who wanted the Nickel Trophy at "home" rather than housed at UND. Mudra and his successor, Ron Erhardt, won national championships in 1965, 1968, and 1969.

## O.A. Stevens, a "modern Audubon"

For more than 70 years, from the time he arrived in 1909, Orin Alva Stevens played a leading role in NDAC-SU life. Although he officially retired in 1956, Stevens made regular daily trips to his office to carry on research and worldwide correspondence until a short time before his death in 1980.

A botanist, Dr. Stevens continued the long line of systematic research on the ecology of North Dakota begun in 1890 by C.B. Waldron and later pursued by Waldron's brother and H.L. Bolley. When NDAC awarded Stevens an honorary Doctor of Science degree in 1948, Dean Walster called him a "natural philosopher, a modern Audubon" for his exhaustive studies of plants, insects and birds on the Northern Plains. His work as a seed analyst and his weed research was also vital to the state's agricultural economy. The University of North Dakota recognized Stevens with the honorary doctorate in 1965.

Dr. Stevens was an original founder and curator of the museum collections for the North Dakota Institute for Regional Studies. This group of NDAC faculty and staff was committed to studying the resources of the region, plant, animal and mineral as well as cultural. Steven's book **Handbook of Plants in North Dakota** was the first book published by the Institute.

In 1967 a new science building was named for Dr. Stevens and

the herbarium with the plant collection curated by him was installed on the top floor. The herbarium contains the 1,200 native plant species known to exist in North Dakota, and it represents the long, patient line of research that began with a few men in 1890.

## Askanase Hall, first in a new direction

When the curtain rose on "Midsummer Night's Dream" at Askanase Hall in 1968, NDSU took an important step in a new direction. The theater became the new home of the Little Country Theatre, and NDSU had built its first building initiated by private money, a gift from former Fargoan Reuben Askanase and his wife Hilda in memory of his parents.

The building worked wonderfully both theatrically and architecturally due in large measure to Fred Walsh, the head of speech and drama. Walsh supplied the acting talent and the actual design plan. The building also roused the Alumni and Development Foundation and the Fargo community to join in an active building program which became known as SU75, a plan initiated by President Loftsgard at his inauguration in 1969. Reuben Askanase became Chairman of the NDSU Development Foundation. Together with Paul "Buck" Gallagher, the President of the Alumni Association, he led the effort which brought about the new construction of other badly needed facilities for physical education, home economics, music and additions to Askanase and Sudro Hall.

Walsh

Askanase and Gallagher

## The strain of war

The strain of the Viet Nam War was evident at NDSU when students picketed a speech by Vice President Hubert Humphrey. Other students remained active in ROTC and some campaigned for George Romney.

## L.D. Loftsgard and the latest chapter

On April 11, 1969, the latest chapter in the University's history began when Laurel D. Loftsgard officially became the tenth President of the University. Loftsgard is the first North Dakotan and graduate of the University to hold that position. Since they first moved into the President's house, Laurel and Carol Loftsgard's children have both received degrees from their father at NDSU Commencement.

The success of any administration depends upon the people around the President. In 1970 these people included David Worden, Vice President for Academic Affairs; Jerry Richardson, Director of Communications; Burt Brandrud, Registrar; Robert Sullivan, Special Projects Director; Art Schultz, Extension Director; Glenn Smith, Dean of the Graduate School; Les Pavek, Dean of Students; Frank Mirgain, Dean of Engineering; Archer Jones, Dean of Arts and Sciences; Ken Gilles, Vice President for Agriculture; James Sugihara, Dean of Chemistry and Physics; Dale Wurster, Dean of Pharmacy; Arlon Hazen, Dean of Agriculture; Don Stockman, Business Manager.

An aerial view of the campus in the 1970s shows a campus changing and spreading northward. Barns have disappeared from near the center of campus, relocated far to the northwest. Dacotah Field and a large New Field House are nearly at Hector Field. Three high-rise dorms break the horizon line, two named for Deans Matilda Thompson and Charles Sevrinson and another for Norm Seim, former Director of Housing. The tin huts, well-known to married students, are gone, replaced by University Village across from the stadium and field house. As an indicator of physical change and growth, NDSU Superintendent of the Physical Plant, Gary Reinke, estimates a thirty per cent increase in building space on campus since 1970.

NDSU has all the people it takes to keep the physical plant of a small city running—painters, carpenters, plumbers, electricians, custodians, boiler tenders, mechanics, police and even a radiation safety officer. This was the physical plant staff in 1985.

Sugihara

# Science and mathematics: A new college emerges

In 1973 the College of Chemistry and Physics merged with several departments from Arts and Sciences to form the College of Science and Mathematics. Dr. James Sugihara became dean of the new college and later Dean of the Graduate School.

Sugihara's successor, John Gruber, once referred to the new college as the "Holy Roman Empire" because the departments were so varied and spread about campus.

The psychologists launched even more heavily into experimental psychology as in this biofeedback experiment.

In physics Dr. James Glass established a doctoral program and a curriculum in engineering physics.

In chemistry, Dr. Philip Boudjouk was credited with one of the twenty most-significant discoveries in 1984 by the American Chemical Society for his work in synthesizing new silicon compounds.

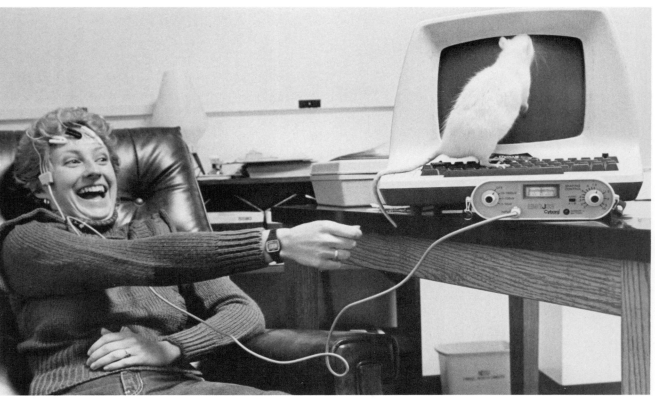

psychology

Glass

Boudjouk

Grier

Stevens Auditorium

Gruber

Zoologist Jim Grier has established a reputation as an expert on animal behavior.

In 1974 geologist John Brophy was at work on the fossil remains of a prehistoric Lake Agassiz creature.

Robert Koob succeeded John Gruber as dean in 1980 and assumed the job of Academic Vice President late in 1984.

Peter Pappas of Polymers and Coatings consulted with NASA on the adhesives used to hold the heat-resistant tiles on the space shuttle Discovery.

Mathematics, under the leadership of Leonard Shapiro, expanded greatly in computer science, statistics and operations research.

Brophy

Koob

Pappas

Shapiro

## Katherine The Great

In 1971 Katherine Burgum reluctantly agreed to become Dean of Home Economics. A 1937 graduate of NDAC, with a master's degree from Columbia, Katherine Burgum was nevertheless new to academia. She was a businesswoman in charge of a large grain and elevator company.

Dean Burgum was less than reluctant, however, about telling the NDSU community about the need for a facility properly suited to the needs of over 1,000 home economics students. A new building, the Family Life Center, appeared on the SU75 building list.

Besides being a builder, Dean Burgum upgraded home economics teaching and research. When she came to the college, three of the faculty held Ph.D. degrees. When she left in 1979, there were nineteen. Substantial funds, previously unavailable from the Agricultural Experiment Station, were also obtained for research in food and nutrition.

Upon her "retirement," Dean Burgum became the President of the NDSU Development Foundation.

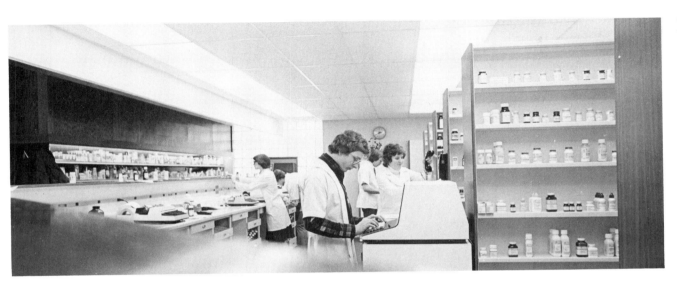

## Pharmacy and the allied health sciences

The College of Pharmacy has grown to include programs in nursing and communication disorders.

Computer terminals are a recent addition to the dispensing lab, but the teaching of Judy Ozbun has been one of the constants in the education of NDSU pharmacists since 1960.

Dean Philip Haakenson returned to teaching pharmacy administration and writing a history of pharmacy in North Dakota in 1980. He was succeeded by Dr. Joseph Norwood of the University of Iowa.

Haakenson

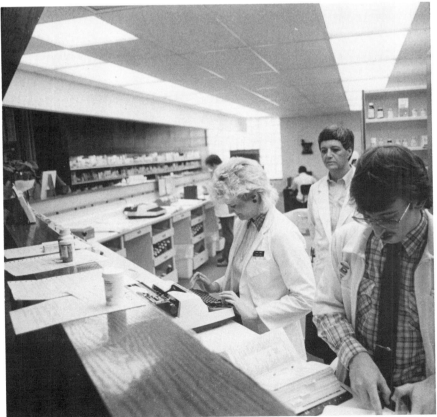

Norwood

## Everyone's bread . . .

The NDSU commitment to agriculture is carried on by new leaders, Myron Johnsrud, Director of Cooperative Extension, and Roald Lund, Dean of Agriculture and Director of the Experiment Station.

In the 1970s facilities dedicated to agriculture expanded and improved. Bacteriology and veterinary science moved to a new Van Es Hall; entomology and animal science occupied a new building named for former president Fred Hultz on the site of old Van Es. A fleet of modern greenhouses was added at the west edge of campus.

Another facility, the Northern Crops Institute, is a regional center for the research and promotion of crops grown in the four-state region of the Dakotas, Minnesota, and Montana.

Lund

Hultz Hall

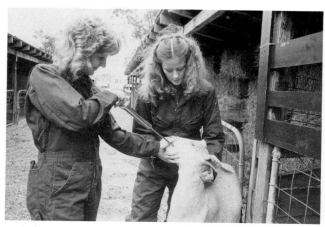

veterinary science

agronomy

greenhouses

Northern Crops Institute

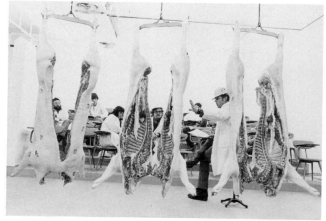

meats lab

By 1984, the slumping North
Dakota farm economy was a
solemn reminder that "our state
is our campus."

## Leading enrollment: The engineers and architects

The architecture faculty used this attention-getting photo of themselves posed on straw bales for an accreditation report in the early 1970s. Architecture students resorted to attention-getting protests in 1978 in order to obtain more studio space. Their demands were met with a renovated quonset once used for aeronautical engineering.

In 1974 the horticulturalists occupied what had been the Dairy Building. When they toyed with the idea of sandblasting the ornament of a cow's head above the entrance of the building into something more appropriate to horticulture, architectural historian Ron Ramsay and his students leapt to the cow's defense by removing it for safe keeping at the Department of Architecture. Speaking of the move to save the cow, Ramsay said, "We couldn't stand by and just watch them blast the symbol of the 'foster mother of the human race' into a rose!"

Stanislao

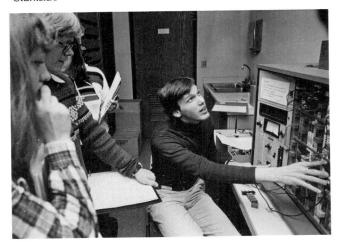

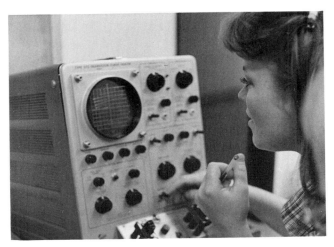

Perkins

When Joseph Stanislao became Dean of the College of Engineering and Architecture in 1975 he faced two problems, according to **Coming of Age:** "The problem in architecture was one of runaway enrollments, an over-extended faculty and a serious shortage of studio space. The problem in engineering was just the opposite—too much space."

The engineering enrollment continued to soar to the point that the college became the largest in the University with over 2,000 students in 1980.

In 1984 the college took a bold step by cooperating with the state of North Dakota and Control Data Corporation to open what will be one of five regional computer centers in the nation with access to worldwide Control Data resources. The center, intended for use by government, private industry, and education, was named for Robert Perkins, a Control Data vice president and a 1942 NDAC graduate in mechanical engineering.

## The humanists and social scientists

When he announced his forthcoming retirement, Dean Archer Jones of the College of Humanities and Social Sciences was the senior dean at the University, having served since 1968. Under Jones, the college strengthened traditional liberal arts majors with improved professional training and a degree track which emphasizes business.

As Director of the North Dakota Institute for Regional Studies, Dean Jones presided over an ambitious publishing effort. A Civil War scholar and military historian, Jones won national recognition for his own books and publications including **How the North Won.**

Despite the trend toward specialization, the humanities and social sciences faculty still come into contact with large numbers of students.

Bill Reid has taught American history to thousands of NDSU students and served as University Archivist. Marillyn Nass has directed Orchesis since 1960 and taught countless ungainly couples to dance in physical education classes.

John Hove was chair of English from 1959-1981.

Warren Kress has taught geography since 1957 and lovingly resurrected a great deal of NDSU history as well.

William Sherman is nationally recognized as an authority on the sociology of the Great Plains.

Reid

Sherman

Jones

Nass

Cater and Holmquist

Jacobsen and Dobitz

Beginning in 1969, Catherine Cater and Delsie Holmquist fostered the NDSU Scholars Program. Dr. Cater was also instrumental in creating the Tri-College Humanities Forum and the humanities major at NDSU.

By 1980, with over 1,000 student majors in business administration and economics, that department aspired to college status. Dean Neil Jacobsen of the College of University Studies and Cliff Dobitz led the department in newly renovated quarters in Putnam Hall.

Poet and writer Richard Lyons taught English from 1952-1981.

Warren Kress has taught geography since 1957 and lovingly resurrected a great deal of NDSU history as well.

John Hove was chair of English from 1959-1981.

Lyons

Kress

Hove

## The Library expands

No sooner had the new Library been constructed than it was filled to capacity both in terms of books and student use. Once again plans were made for more space. The Legislature responded and in 1978 the Library was remodeled, including a large addition which momentarily relieved the space pressure.

The Director of Libraries, Kilbourn Janecek, and his staff looked pleased at the prospect of a new building, but finding books was more than a little difficult for the staff during the transition.

## Pleasure with charity

Those "seditious" folk singers of the late 1960s seem rather tame by comparison with today's punk rockers. Concert-going is now more important than "touch dancing" or even dancing at all.

Students still turn out to help charities, often with marathons.

Chess maintains a devoted following with the guidance of retired professor Steffan Popel, a grand master.

A male beauty pageant in the Memorial Union ballroom during the late 1970s was another sign of changing times.

Morton

## The excitement of winning athletics

For the past twenty years Bison sports fans have been treated to the excitement of winning.

In the fall. 180 football wins, against 45 losses and 2 ties. After national championships in 1964, 1965 and 1969, Don Morton's teams brought home the title in 1983 with runner-up finishes in 1981 and '84. In cross country the men won a national title in 1972. The women's volleyball team has appeared in national tournaments, and consistently maintained national ranking.

In the winter. Erv Inniger's exciting fast break teams set national attendance records in basketball and won the conference in 1981. Amy Ruley's team was host to the national women's basketball tourney in 1979. Coach Arthur "Bucky" Maughan's wrestling teams have compiled a 220, 66, and 7 dual meet record with three second-place finishes and ten individual champions in the national tournament.

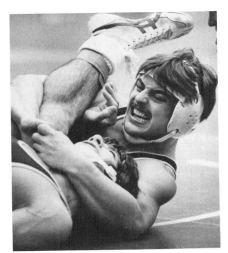

In spring. Don Larson's track teams have won the conference indoor and outdoor titles. NDSU played host to the national outdoor meet in 1978 and the indoor meet in 1985. Sue Patterson's women's track team was the 1984 NCC runnerup after winning cross country and indoor titles.

George Ellis revived the baseball program and led the team back to respectability from 1979-1984.

Athletic Directors Ade Sponberg and Lynn Dorn take pride in running a highly successful, above-the-boards program. Denis Isrow was longtime trainer and "chief of psychology" for Bison teams. Now he serves as head of health, physical education and recreation.

Maughan

Sponberg, Dorn, Isrow

## Fred Walsh and the LCT

From 1952-1980 Fred Walsh was head of speech and drama and the Little Country Theatre. Walsh established a BFA degree in drama and graduate programs in both speech and drama. Askanase Hall, and a sizable addition built in 1977, were largely his design. Walsh also took summer entertainment to the state with the Prairie Stage, a traveling tent theatre.

Recent summer theatre has been on campus with the North Dakota Repertory Theatre.

Fissinger

## Music education and the fine arts

For most of the 1970s NDSU musical organizations campaigned for badly needed new facilities. By 1979 legislative funds, combined with private gifts, enabled the Music Education Center and Festival Concert Hall, both completed in 1981. A major gift from the Reineke Foundation led to the creation of this fine arts complex next to Askanase Hall and the Little Country Theatre.

Dr. Edwin Fissinger is Chair of the Music Department and conducts the NDSU Concert Choir. Fissinger is a nationally recognized arranger, composer, and conductor. Orville Eidem directs the Gold Star Band.

## Farewell, Festival

With the new Music Building, Festival Hall became dispensable. For years crowds had packed the place. Some people liked its "cozy and warm" atmosphere while others believed the building was an embarrassment. It withstood the large crowds and even the tornado.

But finally, after many threats, Festival Hall was scheduled for demolition. Those who would mourn the loss of Festival decided to have one more party in honor of the building. It was, however, to be "a party, not a wake." The people danced to the music of Frank Scott. And then July 19, 1982, the demolition began.

# The long AC/SU line

For many years NDSU Commencement was held in Festival Hall. The faculty donned their robes in Old Main and led an increasingly long line of graduates into that venerable little wooden structure to the satisfaction of proud parents and relatives.

As the line swelled, it moved to what is now called the Old Field House, then Dakotah Field and finally to the New Field House. Women still fan themselves with their programs, men remove their coats, and children squirm in what are still close quarters. Some families cannot resist a spontaneous outburst of approval when their family representative walks across the stage to receive a diploma.

Many of the graduates in this long NDAC/SU line have migrated outward from the state and region. This has always been of concern in North Dakota, but recently in a faculty lecture, agricultural economist Thor Hertsgaard argued that educating our children with the knowledge that many will leave has been profitable economically and socially for the state. Many NDSU families have among them a farmer at home, an engineer or an industrial chemist in another state, perhaps a county agent or home economist somewhere in the region. Likewise others have come to NDSU from neighboring states and more distant points. Some have stayed; others left with a spirit of goodwill demonstrated by their loyalty to the University.

GRADUATION — 1949

In 1890 C.B. Waldron marveled
at the botanical beauty of this
place that became NDAC. Now
a thriving University and
thousands of good lives are
entwined with the beauty of
Waldron's original vision.

*Ho! a cheer for Green and Yellow*
*Up with Yellow and the Green;*
*They're the shades that deck our prairies*
*Far and wide with glorious sheen,*
*Fields of waving green in the spring-time*
*Golden yellow in the fall—*
*How the great high-arching Heaven*
*Looks and laughs upon it all!*

# Index